Skinny in a Straw Hat

Memoir of a Vietnamese American

Hao C. Tran

Thanks for reading my stories, with all my heart.

Hao

AUTON OMOUS PRESS

Aug 23, 2023

ISBN: 978-1-945955-42-6
Epub ISBN: 978-1-945955-43-3

Cover photo by Don Hong Oai (1929–2004).
Interior by Casandra Johns

Contents

Foreword

In this extraordinary debut collection, Hao C. Tran brings a Viet Kieu (Vietnamese sojourner) perspective to the war years as well as their aftermath in Vietnam and the diaspora to anglophone readers—such a needed viewpoint given that our literature and films are almost exclusively concerned with the experience of American veterans. In his exquisitely crafted memoir, Tran recreates the Saigon of his childhood with his leaving to Australia then accidental immigration to the U.S. Interwoven with his stories are those of his brothers who remained, of his brothers who left in boats, of a friend who served in the Vietnamese army in Cambodia, of his father in a re-education camp, and of his mother who bore the burden and the labor of survival. And so much more— this is creative nonfiction at its most powerful, all rendered with incredible attention to detail.

Indeed, Tran's sensitivity to detail makes this collection so much more than a narrative of conflict and struggle. He explores the ecological degradation due to industrialization and deforestation since the war, the complex relations between the government and people, between northerners and southerners, between those who left and those who stayed, between his generation and the next. He paints the vast changes of the city of Saigon and the lives of the people. Even the different ways that the Vietnamese language is spoken is elaborated. Tran's collection opens the reader to entire worlds.

I first read a few of Tran's stories many years ago when he took a memoir class I taught summers at Berkeley City College. We published an earlier version of "Another Tet" in our journal *Milvia Street*. Tran continued in my poetry classes and later began translating lyrics from Vietnamese. And publications of some of this work followed. In early 2020, he emailed me that he'd "been writing stories" and wanted me to look them over. How many pages? Around 150. The shelter-in-place of 2020 afforded me time I rarely have, and as our country spiraled down into violent anti-Asian racism, Tran emailed me story after story, each one opening to a world I could hardly imagine before. It was an honor and a pleasure to do the first wave of revision and edits on this manuscript.

It's important to deeply consider Tran's self-described diasporic position as Viet Kieu. "Viet Kieu" is used mostly in Vietnam to name those who either left or who were born and raised in other countries. Rarely do those of diaspora use this term for themselves. Tran's writing serves to link him back to Viet Nam, acknowledging Vietnamese perspective of him as now an outsider. He's spent far more years speaking more English than Vietnamese and returns "home" as a tourist, longing for the twenty years of absence. Tran's deep voice is one of Viet Kieu *saudade*. Yet his stories do for more than this, for to tell his family's stories to an anglophone audience is another bridge he's decided to cross.

For his generation, Tran says, writing is less a focus than is making new lives: his brothers know what they went through.

Certainly, to tell these stories may also release many difficult emotions as well. But for his nieces and nephews both in America and Vietnam, "they want to know," Tran stresses. It's important to keep in mind that often trauma and displacement are followed by years of silence. When a few writers break that silence, an out-pouring of personal stories flow. Something to consider as you delve into this book.

Sharon Coleman, 20 January 2023, Berkeley, California

Introduction

"Vietnam is a woman, a long-suffering mother," my history teacher pointed at the map on the high school wall. "Look at her: up north, the mountainous border is a conical straw hat to keep her safe from China's endless assaults. Her thin neck is a stretch of sand between the Pacific Ocean and the Ho Chi Minh Trail along the mountain range. Her belly is the central highland that has been the home of many tribes, now taken over by colonial greed for coffee and tea plantations. The Mekong Delta is the rice basket that barely feeds the whole country. Look again: she is doubled over from all this pain and sorrow of war."

I left Vietnam as a young man to go to college in Australia and later settled in the United States. Shortly after I left, the war ended, and I couldn't return for twenty years. Since 1994, I have come back to my homeland a dozen times. These stories are based on my journeys.

This book is about a Việt Kiều—a Vietnamese living overseas—looking for his home after twenty years. A Việt Kiều belongs neither here nor there. A Việt Kiều is not Vietnamese anymore because he lost his citizenship by leaving. He also is not a foreigner who is treated with respect and indifference. He is considered among the lucky ones to get out alive and live his dreams in a rich country. He is welcome to visit and spend dollars, but he is no longer part of the tribe. He will leave again because his home is no longer the village.

This collection of short stories is about the rice fields, water buffaloes, and mangos. It is about the water hyacinths, native grass, lotus flowers, scents of plumeria, and egrets and cranes returning to a restored wetland in the Mekong. It is for the landless refugees with no place to go. It travels across the ocean that separates those who left and those left behind.

Ghosts—dead and alive—inhabit the rice fields, jungles, and hot dusty villages. They haunt me and make me write their stories.

These pages are love letters to the skinny woman in a straw hat.

Skinny Woman in a Straw Hat

From the clear blue sky, we descended into billowing clouds, white cotton balls that rose like trees in tropical rainforests. Through the bulbous canopy, the plane dropped, and a collective gasp erupted from the passengers. Hundreds of traveling Việt Kiềus uttered a loud guttural "WHOA" when they saw the land below: green patches of rice paddies, thatched huts, sporadic tombs, coconut and banana trees, all so peaceful.

Sitting next to me, a woman in her late sixties was sobbing as she kept checking her passport and the many duplicate forms that we all had to fill out, declaring place of birth, itemized gifts, how much money we carried into the country, and the entry visa that we had got from a consulate in Bangkok.

"Can you help me with this? Do I have everything in order?" She asked me to look at her pile of papers. "I have not been back since *Giải Phóng*, I have to see my mother. She is ninety-two now, and this may be my last chance."

I was among the Việt Kiềus on the plane returning for the first time, twenty years since *Giải Phóng*, the liberation of the South.

The Việt Kiều called the event the Fall of Saigon or *Mất Nước* to label the loss of their homeland.

"Young man, how did you escape?" she asked.

"I was not a refugee," I explained. "I was already a foreign student in Australia. I wasn't there when *Giải Phóng* happened." "Lucky you," she said. "You should have nothing to fear. My late husband was a policeman before." Việt Kiều always referred to their lives as before and after *Giải Phóng*. "He died recently, so I am traveling alone," she wiped her eyes again. "He would not come back anyway because he was afraid they would detain him."

The old Saigon policemen back then were brutal and corrupt, the best that money could buy, we often joked. I had often been stopped by men in khaki uniforms waving batons when I was riding my bike home from school. They checked my ID for age, where I lived, and whether or not I should be in the military already. Even though I had all the documents, they would make up a fine for me to pay right on the spot. They got the wrong guy since I never had any money in my wallet. "Go!" they waved me off like a fly. Those were just traffic cops. The higher the level, the larger the bribes. Anyone who had control of your time, your money, or your life got you by the throat.

"We are approaching Saigon," the pilot said calmly. It was obvious he didn't say Ho Chi Minh City. Even after twenty years since the city had been renamed by the government in Hanoi, most Vietnamese in the south and expatriates still called it Saigon, the pilots did the same out of respect for the people on the plane. "Please remain seated until we are safely on the ground." Too late. The Việt Kiều had already unbuckled and fought for a window view of the sprawling concrete city. "Please, Please!" the flight attendants pleaded. The plane rocked and slammed down hard on the tarmac. "Welcome home to Tân Sơn Nhất Airport," the pilot exhaled.

My friends were stunned. They witnessed a chaotic scene that they had never seen in their entire Midwestern life. Harold couldn't say a simple "wow!" Gordon remained motionless while Deb searched for her Canon A1. Around them, old people were choking up, trembling with passports clutched tightly in their hands, many faces distorted with open mouths. The cabin smelled of sweat and bad breath. The aisle was crammed with bodies fighting to get off the plane.

A few months before this trip, Deb called me up. "Let's go to Vietnam," she always sounded cheerful. "A bunch of us are volunteering for the International Crane Foundation with the mission to restore the crane habitat in the Mekong Delta. We need you. Let's go together, and you can help us as our interpreter. I would love to meet your family too."

"Yes, but I can only be with you for one week. I have family business to tend to." I had waited a long time to make this trip, and it was a coincidence that I could have the company and support of some friends. I wasn't sure if I was ready to make this reentry alone.

I left Saigon one year before *Giải Phóng,* right after high school graduation. I was a recipient of a scholarship to go to college overseas. The Colombo Plan was a generous gift by the Australian government to educate promising Vietnamese kids so they could return and help with post-war restoration. I was among the lucky ones chosen that year. I had no idea that leaving Vietnam was the event that would shape the rest of my life and the person I would become.

Giải Phóng put an end to the war on April 30, 1975, and South Vietnam was no more. In one day, the refugees and I became citizens of no country. My father was sent to a labor camp up north. Ma and my brothers were evicted from their home and taken to a remote area near the Cambodian border to start a farm life in a new economic zone. Boat people, many of whom were in the military or had worked closely with the U.S., were being victimized by the new regime. They risked their lives in the open sea, hoping to find land before they sank, ran out of food and water, or were raped and killed by pirates. For nearly ten years, tens of thousands of refugees arrived in camps in Hong Kong, Malaysia, or the Philippines. The rest died along the way.

I watched the fall of Saigon from afar, through television news and information from the South Vietnam embassy. I tried to reach my parents during the chaos, but it was hopeless. Then we lost contact altogether for years before I could reconnect with Ma through a contact I had in France. "Don't come home," Ma wrote on a piece of paper hidden in a reused envelope that somebody smuggled out of the country. "Your father is in a re-education camp in the North. We need money, so please send us fifty dollars, only if it is safe." It was always the same news from home every few months. "Please send help but don't come home. I may never see you again, but I will always love you. Don't worry, take care of yourself, study hard, my dear son."

After *Giải Phóng*, it had always been expected that Hanoi would punish the people in the South, especially the military and collaborators with Americans. All the factories, roads, and bridges had been destroyed. The Vietnamese government exported all farm products to repay China and the Soviets for their debts, and the people starved. The ten years following Saigon's fall were remembered as the Hunger Years. What I couldn't understand was the embargo the U.S. imposed on Vietnam for twenty years.

This was a kick in the head when their opponent was already on their knees.

It took two decades for the U.S. government to begin the healing process. Following Perestroika and Glasnost in the Soviet Union, Hanoi followed suit with "Đổi Mới," literally a policy change to something new, a new openness for the market economy. Vietnam sent the signal to the world that the country was open for business and that expatriates were welcome to return home to visit. Almost twenty years after the last U.S. personnel left Vietnam, President Clinton lifted the embargo, restored diplomatic relations, and started the process of normalizing trade with Vietnam. Việt Kiềus began to return en masse.

"Thank you for being part of the team," Deb said when we met up in Wisconsin to begin our journey. "I am so glad to have you. You are Vietnamese and speak the language. We feel safer with you as our guide."

"I don't know, Deb," I frowned. "I am a Việt Kiều now. I am neither American nor Vietnamese. They won't do anything to you because you are Americans. Funny that after they beat you, they still fear you. And me? I am not sure how they will treat me. Việt Kiềus are fair game."

I had spent more years outside Vietnam than I lived there as a kid. I had become more American than I was Vietnamese. I could speak both languages with equal ease, but my thoughts and dreams had been in English. I was born in Vietnam but became a citizen of another country. I was going to return to Vietnam, not as a native son but as a guest—hopefully, a welcome one.

The Vietnam I knew was full of death. One war followed another, and it was hard to tell when one ended and another began. I was thirteen years old when war came close to home. We woke up on the day of Tết in 1968 to the sounds of guns and rockets as gun fights broke out in the streets of Saigon. Planes were dive-bombing a few blocks away from our house. My dad was not home while Ma rushed us to seek shelter at her sister's house in a safer neighborhood. I saw dead bodies in gutters, a foot was hanging from a lamppost, people were running and screaming, kids in their arms.

The year after Tết, Americans made sure we had enough guns and armed men and boys to defend our city in what they called the Strategic Village campaign. I was made to spend one night a week at the neighborhood police station for gun training. The hard bamboo bed was full of bed bugs, and mosquitoes had teeth. They gave kids real guns and live ammunition. I was assigned an old Carbine rifle left over from WWII with a heavy and beautiful wooden rifle stock. It was an awesome piece of art, and I could take it apart and put it back together, but I never fired a shot. Some local kids had blown their feet off.

I had developed a phobia for guns, and it didn't matter what kind or who wielded them. I believe that people with guns usually do more harm than good. I could have died one day when my older brother Bê and I were walking down a dirt trail near the house. He spotted a ripening durian fruit hanging over a fence and couldn't resist its wafting smell. "Hurry," he broke it off and carried it like a baby. "Let's go home."

A skinny kid appeared with a gun from the big house behind the gate. "Hey, you thieves! It's mine. Give it back!" The rifle was longer than he was tall and half rusted out. I stared at the nozzle, as big as the black of his eyes. I wasn't sure if it was loaded and whether or not he could shoot, but he had his finger on the trigger. "Brother Bê, let's return it," I begged meekly. My brother was not going to give up easily, and suddenly, the kid shot at us. "BANG!"

The explosion was deafening. He missed. We dropped the fruit and ran. Like hell, we ran.

Terrorist attacks were common. Movie theaters, marketplaces, and schools were easy targets. The years after Tết of 1968, the shelling into Saigon continued. In the night, the sound of a missile pierced the still air "ZHEEE..." for a few seconds, and then an explosion somewhere in the city. Sometimes far, sometimes close. The next day, on the radio news, I would find out a church or a slum neighborhood had been hit, with dozens of casualties. People got killed while they slept, adults and kids; it didn't matter. Death came randomly, like the lottery, raining down through the tin roofs.

Years passed, and I had not thought about the fear of death. Instead, I was overwhelmed with homesickness for my family and the land. In Canberra, there was only one Chinese restaurant, and every now and then, I skipped the dorm's cafeteria food and went out for a plate of fried rice. It was just a heaping serving of greasy rice with bites of BBQ pork and green peas flavored in soy sauce, and yet it was heavenly. I missed everything about the greenness of the swaying palms and the wet rice fields, the heavy rain that beat on the tin roof like a drum, and the cicada songs of summer while the flame trees bloomed. I missed Ma's home-cooked meals.

Ma had written to me a few weeks before this trip home, "Con Xê, in a few days, I will be there outside the gate. Look for me where you and I parted long ago. I am much older now. I am frail, and my hair is all white. I will look like the many mothers, but you will recognize me. I thank heaven for my chance to see my son again, you who live so far away." I tucked the letter in my journal, my travel companion, along with rolls of Kodachrome. I wanted to write everything, record every moment, every second.

Often, I searched my memory for her image, and she was always in black and white, just like in the photos I had carried with me for twenty years. In them, she was a young woman before she married my father: a shy teenager with big front teeth standing next to her older sister, who should have married before she did. She was leaning on my father on their honeymoon in Da Lat, both looking at a distant future out of the corner of the frame. I had a picture of her holding a chubby baby with a round face and legs full of dimples. She smiled so proudly at the camera as if to say to my father taking the picture, "Look! He is a healthy, happy boy. He eats everything and is so easy to please. He never gets sick." She had told me many times that I had a strong immune system because I fed on her milk and refused to drink Borden condensed milk. The last picture taken was when she stood with me at Tân Sơn Nhất Airport in her best *Áo Dài*. She wore dark sunglasses, so I couldn't see her eyes. I don't know which one of us was braver, me going out alone into the world or her letting go of a piece of her heart. I told her I would be back in four years after completing the scholarship program. She told me to take good care of myself and not to worry about anyone back home. She held my arm for as long as she could, stroked my hair, kissed me on the forehead, and pushed me through the gate.

My world had changed so much. I was no longer the eighteen-year-old boy who left Tân Sơn Nhất airport with a small bag with a few shirts and pants, songbooks, and twenty dollars from my father, his last month's pay. I was now almost forty and had a family of my own. I had become a citizen of America, enjoying all the freedoms that I never had before. I had worked hard to gain the necessary skills and qualifications for a middle-class lifestyle, a townhouse in the suburbs, and a Toyota Camry. I wore a suit, read the papers while on the Metro to work, and spent weekdays in an air-conditioned office. I traveled all over the country and managed scientists and their projects. I could speak and write English better than I could my native tongue, which I only used at home. I was hailed as the role model of a successful minority in America, one who started as an immigrant and had become a high-level official in the federal government.

Before I left Saigon, I was a frog looking up from the bottom of a well, and my view of the world was a small circle of sunlight above. All I knew was my family and a few high school friends. My dad gave me an old Goebel bicycle and half a liter of gas each month that he got from his army supplies. There was never any pocket money for me, and I didn't need any. The bike gave me the freedom to go on short excursions with friends. We often took a day trip to an orphanage in *Gò Vấp* to help the nuns, went swimming in a river, and sometimes sat around in a field under the shade of the coconut palms singing songs with the old guitar an aunt gave me.

Since then, my world expanded to a wide-angle perspective, new ideas, free-thinking, and open questions. In twenty years, I had already added another lifetime to my age. My mind was loaded with layers of new data on top of old storage. My new memories and experiences covered up the distant past before I left Saigon like new coats of paint. Still, like the silver particles in old photographs, some images don't fade no matter how much aging time did to the body and mind. The imprints call us back to where we were born, like salmon finding their stream of birth, like migratory birds returning to their nesting site.

The cabin door finally opened. The hot and humid air invaded the air-conditioned interior like a fog. The Việt Kiềus fought their way to the exit door and stumbled down the steel stairways to the steaming tarmac. There we waited like cattle for a rusty old bus to take us to the main terminal in the distance.

As we got off the plane, the policeman's widow kept a short distance in front of us. She walked just a few steps before us as if she found safety in a young Việt Kiều traveling with American friends.

"Just stick with us," I said to her. "We will make sure you get to the other side."

I looked around. The runway hadn't improved much since the day I left Saigon, except for more coats of asphalt. Alongside, no grass had grown on the red dirt. The U.S. defoliated around airports and military bases to create defensible space, so much and the toxins so persistent that nothing could grow for decades. Quonset huts and abandoned concrete bunkers lined both sides of the bare runway. Tân Sơn Nhất airport terminal hadn't changed much either: a moldy concrete building with a lettering sign on top, one gate for arrival and one for departure. Twenty years earlier, I left this runway for Australia with plans to return after four years of college. Months later, on the same runway, many South Vietnamese crammed into the last airplanes and helicopters while the airport was being shelled, leaving behind the city engulfed in fire and smoke.

I was now standing again on Vietnam soil. I had returned to the outstretching arms of the skinny woman in the straw hat, the image my history teacher in high school had sketched in my head. She was an S-shaped country with the northern end shaped like a conical straw hat, her back the long, rugged sea coast that formed her bent-over spine, the green foggy hills of the Central Highlands were her aching belly, and the rich fertility of the Mekong Delta that fed the people. I had longed to return to this narrow strip of land on the planet earth like a migratory bird searching for his roosting place.

Inside the belly of the terminal, mosquitoes attacked us. The smell of urine and feces overwhelmed us. My friends and I were at the back of the crowd. The Vietnamese had never believed in getting in lines, but I expected more courtesy from Việt Kiềus, who should have learned better habits in lawful countries. No, they reverted right back as soon as they landed on native land. I forgave them. They, too, had to cross the portal to the other side where loved ones awaited, where they were before they took to the air or the sea, leaving all behind.

"I am glad I am taking Lariam," Harold exclaimed. We chuckled at his dry humor. My friends and I had taken precaution against Malaria: One pill a week, one before the trip and several to follow. We were heading to a remote area in the Mekong Delta later on this trip. We followed the crowd through the passport and customs gates. Our lady companion got into a long discussion with a scowling official in a green uniform. He asked many questions while looking through her many sheets of paperwork. He barked at her while she kept wiping her nose with tissue papers. I saw her slip a twenty-dollar bill in her passport, and he waved her on without cracking a smile. We were next.

Gordon boldly stepped in front of us with Deb right behind him. Harold was behind me and his head was above the rest of the crowd. It was clear my friends were protecting me as we presented our paperwork. The official tried to ask a couple of questions in broken English, and he finally gave up. He looked at me with a half smile and nodded. We were done with the inspection.

We found the lady again in the crowd going through customs.

"I am now going to the village, half a day from here. My brother is waiting for me out there. Thank you, young man, and I hope you find your family too." She smiled with relief.

Two hours after landing on the tarmac, we found ourselves on the other side of the portal. The Việt Kiềus ahead of us had already pushed and bribed their way through. Deb pulled out her camera and shot away at the crowd outside the building. A steel barricade stood between those arriving and the people waiting outside in the midday sun. The stream of Việt Kiềus merged into the waiting crowd like a river entering the sea with the smoothness of an estuary. Both came together, a fluid reunion of two worlds. Soon, I would join that river, enter the sea, and connect the two pieces of my life, before and after *Giải Phóng*.

Outside the gate, people were weeping, hugging, and screaming. They pulled away in groups, away from the barricade towards the shading tamarind trees, they shouted their questions and greetings that they had stored for so many years. They wanted to know what happened in each other's lives, who lived, who died. "Wow!" Harold uttered his usual impression. He came to see the cranes in the Mekong but this scene was much more amazing. He had his large hand on my back to calm me the entire time. "Now go look for your mom." He gave me a push. "I will watch your stuff. Go out there, my friend."

Deb gave me the stems of orchid flowers she had bought from Bangkok. "Please give this to your Mom," she smiled.

"Đi gì mà như ăn cướp?" A guard insulted me as I hurried out the gate. When I grew up here, being called a robber was extremely hurtful. I didn't care. I was too eager to find Ma.

I ventured into the blinding sunlight. The hot concrete pad outside the barricade was where we said goodbye twenty years earlier. Ma had held me one last time before she sent me away to another world. She wanted me to live a better life without war and hunger, even though she would not be in it. She wanted me to go to college, to find love and perhaps one day to return when peace was truly at hand.

The crowd had thinned. The river of people had merged into the ocean and I found myself standing, looking left and right. *What would she look like? What if she would not recognize me at all? What if I couldn't?*

I looked for a woman in a silk *Áo Dài*, in her forties, eyes behind large sunglasses, the Ma I had said goodbye to twenty years earlier. I looked for the pillar she had leaned against when I turned away and took off in a large airplane for a long trip all around the world. *I am here now Ma, where are you?* Then I saw an older woman in a brown tunic, her hair white, her face dark and wrinkled, her bony hands grasping the strap of a peasant straw hat. She looked at me but did not move. Our eyes locked. Hers asked: *"Is that you? Is this real? Con Xê?"* Then she stepped toward me, and I ran to meet her.

I had found my mother again. I had come home again. I had found the skinny woman in the straw hat.

Through the Lens

He wore a crooked and toothless smile. Half of his face—no eye, no cheek, just folds of skin the color of dirt—sank into his skull. His one eye spoke to me in a foreign language.

His contorted body slithered along the sidewalk pavement littered with spit and cigarette butts. His tattooed arm propelled his body forward. The other ended in a stub just below the elbow. The atrophied legs trailed behind the bundle of his body of no more than sixty pounds, mostly bones and rags.

Through the lens, he came in and out of focus. The horizontal line in the middle of the ground glass circle split him in halves as I struggled to compose the shot. My hands shook, and my heart raced. This could be an award-winning shot: a broken warrior begging for a living against the backdrop of high-rise buildings in a new postwar Vietnam.

A decisive moment for a hunter—the prey was in the crosshairs, the gun cocked—yet I couldn't pull the trigger. *Should I press the shutter?* He smiled again, challenging me to get it over with. He wanted me to do what other tourists had done before: documenting his misery and putting a dollar in the crook of his arm so that he could go on begging.

I, a Việt Kiều, sat outside a café in the posh Ho Chi Minh city downtown, gawking at passers-by. An ocean of experiences separated us. I could be him and he could be me had we gone down each other's path thirty years back. Now, we were staring at each other from opposite ends of a Canon lens.

Sometimes, I still kick myself for not pushing the button that would set off a chain reaction: the mirror flips up with a solid thud, the diaphragm blades spring open to let light flood into the chamber and burn his image on Kodachrome. I could have stored his image for the remainder of my days, made copies to prove that I was there, and even won a photo contest.

His dignity was not for me to take; his life story belonged to him alone; his losses should remain his and he didn't have to sell them to me for a dollar.

I reached in my pocket for the remainder of my cash, and without counting, I walked closer to him, knelt down with my knees on the sharp pavement, opened his dirty pants pocket, and stuffed the money in there. I walked away, camera hanging at my side. His face, his eye, his clothes, his broken body seared into my mind.

500 Miles

The last year of high school before I left Vietnam for Australia, I was a skinny and anxious teenager like a million others who grew up there during the war. Many had gone to the front and died or returned without arms or legs. Our parents worried daily about what would happen to their sons. They did their best to send them to college in hope of deferments. Wealthy people bribed government officials to falsify IDs, buy positions to avoid combat duties; some even hid their sons behind priesthood. They paid for their children to go overseas if they could, but that cost a fortune, and only very few rich people could pull it off.

I went to an all-boys public school in Gia Dinh, a suburb of Saigon. We were lucky enough to have a free education. I had a handful of close friends—we studied together, ate together, and hung together. We shared our worries and our germs. Tài was fiercely competitive and always stayed at the top of the class. His idealistic plan was to become president of South Vietnam after making a fortune in business. Khanh was timid and constantly worried about his ma and siblings. His father had been killed in the Tết Offensive five years before, and now, as the oldest son, he bore the heavy responsibility for his family. Soon he would be drafted because he was born a year before us. Bình and I really had no clues at all about what to do with our lives, although Bình was more vocal about his plans.

"I am going to sign up and fight for South Vietnam," he said often. "You are going to take care of my mom if something happens to me, right? Promise me that."

"Sure, you will take care of my mom too if I die before you, right?" I replied, knowing there was no way either of us could.

He talked about leading troops, fighting their way to win the war and restore peace to the country. In fact, his eyesight was so bad I wondered if the army would even take him. His glasses were as thick as the bottom of a Coke bottle, and he held books six inches in front of his nose to read. However, with that crazy idea in mind, he abandoned all schooling. It seemed just an excuse to stop doing homework, cut classes, and hang out with other students who didn't care about school and were failing to earn good grades. They were surely going to war, so what was the point of learning algebra and memorizing biology lessons? They spent their time around the girls' school to pick off the rebels for dates. Their parents were very worried but helpless. Bình's mom kept telling me to help him come back to "the righteous path" but who was I to change his mind?

I was the studious one. Not because I had a better plan but because I didn't have the guts to try anything else. My only plan was to play it by the books, literally. I was the model student, getting straight A's, passing exams, and following the paths of the elders in my clan to become a teacher, government worker, an engineer, having a salary, and then a family. Other than my maternal grandfather, who was a merchant from Canton, none of my ancestors knew how to make money from commerce, farming, or any craft.

Becoming a scholar was the only path that my family knew.

My more studious friends improved their English however they could. We all knew that English proficiency was needed if we were going to make a living. Many Vietnamese were working for the Americans already, and they earned good salaries. They worked for the American embassy, corporations with questionable portfolios, and military contractors. As an officer for the military in South Vietnam, my father worked with American troops in "communications" although I didn't know exactly what that meant. Occasionally, he invited some American friends to our home in the army base to drink beer. "My sons, I have seven sons," his laughter rang through the house. Although Ma always wished for a daughter and kept making baby girls' clothes and chose a flowery name every time she got pregnant, the outcome remained the same: another boy. My father couldn't care less and was proud of the fact that he ran a boy-making factory. "Let me show you how," he joked every time someone asked him about the near impossible odds of siring seven boys in a sexist society.

The best place to learn English in Saigon was Hội Việt Mỹ, the Vietnamese American Association, a collaboration between a U.S. university and Vietnamese business tycoons. It was a reputable organization and offered classes taught by English-speaking teachers. They were far better than my local high school teachers, who could barely pronounce the words correctly because they had only learned them from books without real practice with the language.

I never asked my parents to pay for Hội Việt Mỹ because I knew they had no money for that. My friends who were poor like me told me about learning English by going to the Tin Lành Church. *Tin Lành* is Vietnamese for the Christian Missionary Alliance that sent people to Vietnam to evangelize, and they did a good job of converting many to Christianity. Although my family belongs to a minority of Catholics in a Buddhist country, I was already losing interest in God with so many unanswered questions. *Why was this war happening? Why us? Why did so many have to die?* The Church offered an English class at night, and Titus Peachey was the teacher. They charged a small fee that paid for his salary. Bình signed up but rarely showed up for class. Although the fee was much lower than Hội Việt Mỹ, I had no money to sign up.

It was through Chị (older sister) Nga that I got into Titus's class. She was in her forties, ruddy and tall for Vietnamese women. You could tell she was from the countryside from the way she talked, very direct and with simple words. She worked for the World Vision, and they paid her a decent salary relative to what Vietnamese normally made.

"You are a good student." She approached me after church one day.

"Thank you, Chị Nga. How do you know?" I looked at her big feet.

"I could tell by the way you learn. Very fast. I have to look at the words in the hymn book because I can't remember them."

Then she asked me if I could help her with the translation of some documents: financial aid applications to send to World Vision. I always loved a challenge, so I said yes. My spoken English was very limited, but my vocabulary was decent with *English for Today* book learning, so I translated the letters for her. The translations were not difficult; they were all the same: "We live in the village of .... I have five children...My husband is dead...We wish to start a chicken (or pig) farm and need one hundred dollars to get started." She offered to pay me, but I declined.

My mother raised me in a very old-fashioned way. She cared a lot about appearance, and military officers like my father were a proud lot. Being able to provide for their family was a matter of honor, so Ma always warned me, "No, you can't work. Your goal is to focus on school and then you will find a decent living when you graduate from college." I knew the world had changed, and my father could not support seven sons. Ma found work wherever she could to supplement his paycheck. She raised chickens in the back of the house even though the feather dust worsened her asthma. She converted the front of the house to a mini-mart selling aspirin, candies, feminine pads, homemade popsicles, and even cigarettes in singles.

I could not help Ma, but at least I could help myself. Chị Nga asked me if I could tutor her two girls. They needed help with math, and she knew I was an A student in algebra, trigonometry, and physics. "My mom doesn't allow me to work," I told Chị Nga.

"Why don't we do this? You teach my kids, and I will pay your tuition for the English class," she offered me a deal I could not turn down. There was no money changing hands, so I could tell Ma honestly that I did not work for money.

Each week, I spent one evening at Chị Nga's house to tutor her two girls to solve simultaneous equations and one evening in Titus' English class. The girls had a hard time with the concepts of x and y and how to deal with two equations and two unknowns. Chị Nga knew that progress was slow, but she kept the deal and as long as I showed up, she was happy.

The English class was much different from the way we learned in our public school. I didn't repeat line by line after the teacher. I didn't have to translate from English to Vietnamese and back again. Titus didn't use *English for Today* that I had learned by heart. He talked to us just the way one would talk to a friend.

Titus was a tall man. Really tall. He must have been more than six feet, but then it was hard to tell because I had never seen anyone that tall before. He had blond hair, a narrow face and very long front teeth. He rode a Vespa and had no girlfriends, at least I never saw him with one. He seemed so awkward with all his long bones in a classroom of short and underfed students, who were there to learn any word that came out of his mouth.

The English class was not large, maybe fifteen students. I was shy as were most kids in Vietnam. We were not brought up in a society where people are encouraged to express opinions. At home, we never said "no" to our parents. At school, we never asked questions. What we learned we did from books: we memorized all the lessons and recited them back line by line, word by word, commas and all. The best minds were tested by their ability to repeat what they were given the week before. One aspect worked really well though: for me, it taught me the discipline and skill that I still have today when it comes to memorization. However, it never fostered creativity or problem solving, skills I had to learn when I left home and lived in societies very different from Vietnam.

Titus didn't ask us to memorize anything. He didn't even have handouts. It was always an hour and a half conversation. It was participatory. Almost like judo or theater games, exploration, learning by doing and with a partner.

"Good evening! What's your name?"

"My name is Hao," I pronounced carefully.

"Just like '*How* do you do?'" he asked.

"It is H A O, with a ` above the A. Not How. It is Ha`o."

"What does it mean?"

"It means good, but more than good. It means many things."
My English was not enough to give him all the nuances.

"I know you are good, Hao. You are a good son. You are a good person and you are a good friend," he nodded.

For three weeks in a row, I had not seen Bình. Normally, he would come by to get me to go for a spin on our bikes and share a loaf of Bánh Mì. He even skipped Titus's evening class altogether. I went to his house, but he was not there. His mother was worried and asked me to talk him into coming back to school. "You may find him with his buddies near the Judo school."

I went to the dojo and sure enough, he was drinking coffee and smoking with a few guys at the street corner. He grinned when he saw me. "Did my mother send you here?"

"Yes, what happened? You disappeared."

"Where are *you* these days? You have been so busy in the evenings. I don't see you much anymore." He crushed the cigarette with his flip flop.

I explained to him I had a sort of a job and I am spending a lot of time learning English.

We took a moment to let it soak in. Neither of us found anything to say. We stood under the tamarind tree listening to the cicadas buzzing their crescendo in the summer heat. We had started to drift apart. He was to become a warrior and would survive on his brute strength and street smarts. I would be a teacher or scholar. And the two of us would be friends without being together anymore. Even at that age, we knew.

That evening I went to Titus's class alone. I was not in the mood to talk.

"What have you done today?" he asked me, sensing something was not right.

"Oh, I went to school. I don't know... nothing much. When I finish my homework, I play a few songs. I have a guitar my aunt gave me," I dodged any probing.

"What songs do you sing?"

"Vietnamese songs, folk songs, love songs."

From then on he asked me more questions about Vietnamese music, the composers, what they say, what they write, and how I felt about the songs.

I told him as much as I knew about the songs I liked. Popular Vietnamese music was borrowed from the French, and the French romantic spirit infused our sound and lyrics. I loved the *Tiền Chiến* music my parents listened to, the music *written before the war*, so called, although there was no clear sign of war beginning or ending where we lived. However, the pre-war music was beautiful and haunting, about unrequited love, a wanderer longing for home, the love of a mother who waits for her son to return from afar, and a few boleros and tangos to dance to. The music of my time was sadder, more about war, death, tragic losses, and hopelessness.

My English couldn't describe to Titus all I wanted to say. He saw my frustration and put a gentle hand on my shoulder.

"I love music too. I have a guitar. Let's play together sometime—oh, who is your favorite composer?"

"Trịnh Công Sơn." He was a contemporary composer who wrote anti-war songs disguised in love themes and poetic lyrics. I had collected all his works but the compilation "Ca Khúc Da Vàng," (Songs of the Yellow Race) was the most R-rated in its explicit depiction of the atrocities of our time. In its introduction, he wrote: "All is broken, shattered. The screaming has coalesced to a whispering lament for the fate of Vietnam, a voice arising from bomb craters. To my dear friends who died on mountains and valleys. To the humans who transformed to a gaping wound.

Death becomes a meaningless symbol… Let's gather all the flares in the sky to make a torch, burn away demons, warm the insane in the winter cold."

With government censorship against anti-war music, musicians stuck to romantic music, songs that lament lost love, and at the very worst, about men being away from home fighting for freedom. Only Trịnh Công Sơn gave us what he truly felt, the way we felt. How he got away with that was beyond me.

His music was irresistible to us kids, the generation that had no future. Some people accused him of being subversive and working for the other side. I tried to explain that to Titus.

"Can you translate one for me?" he asked. "Consider that a class assignment."

"OK," I said. In school, I learned to translate literally, word for word. Since I started learning from Titus, I had discovered that it made no sense most of the time to go from one language to another in that fashion. Besides, many idiomatic expressions in each language have no equivalent at all. So, I decided to use the simplest words and focus on the meaning of what Trịnh Công Sơn said in his lyrics. It took a few days, but I finished and it looked like this:

When Peace Comes
(translation of "Tôi Sẽ Đi Thăm by Trịnh Công Sơn)

When peace comes,
I will visit deep tunnels under the village,
city streets littered with craters.

I will look for friends
in cemeteries with gravestones
like straw mushrooms.

When peace comes,
mothers will climb bald mountains
to search for bones.

When the killing stops
children will sing forgotten folk songs
in village streets.

When peace comes,
I will walk from Saigon to the central highlands,
from Hanoi to the South.

When peace comes,
I will join the march for hope
and hope to forget our past.

"Thank you for this, Hao, I had no idea anyone can write a song like this and not get in trouble with the government." Titus kept staring at the poem. "Incredible man!"

I didn't realize that in 1967, even before the Tết Offensive, before the anti-war movement in the U.S. peaked, the children of Vietnam had already been singing these heart-breaking lines.

"I want you to sing it for me sometime, okay?" I agreed.

A few weeks later, Titus showed me a copy of the *Mennonite Newsletter*, the poem was published in Ohio. My name was printed as the translator. Later in life, I authored dozens of publications in scientific journals for the research that I did as a Forest Service scientist, and had a few poems and short stories published in various literary journals, but I will never forget how proud I was then that my name was out there in America. My first publication—it was like a first kiss.

I had found a new passion to excel with English. Titus told me that an average American had a vocabulary of five thousand words. I bought a small dictionary and learned it by heart. Then I moved up to the *Webster's New World* version, which was more than one inch thick. I tore off a few pages a day, carried them in my back pocket to learn in my spare time, and memorized all the irregular verbs backwards and forwards.

While I studied, worked for Chị Nga, and went to English classes at night, my friend Bình spent his time with his gang and got into fights with other tough kids. They fought over girls, over turf, over any provocation the other youth gangs threw at them.

One day, he came to get me at my house and we went to a nearby café to split a *Bánh Mì*. Just like old times, I was hoping. Afterwards, we rode together to an alley within a labyrinth of alleys. I had never been there before and thought that he wanted to introduce me to his girlfriend.

"You wait right here. Don't leave. I will be back in a bit. If I don't come out in five minutes, come and help me." He walked into the alley with a galvanized pipe. I sat on his bike waiting. Three minutes later, he came out smiling with a bruised lip. "Done!" he said.

From then on, I refused to go out with him again. He was so angry with me that he wrote me a letter, the first one ever: "Hao, we have been friends, the best of friends. I can't believe that it has come to this. All you care about is Titus Peachey. Please think how different we were together three years ago and the last three days."

I didn't reply and he never came by again to get me for our daily ride to school. He kept away from me, until the day I left Saigon to go overseas.

My English was improving quickly with Titus. He taught me new words, idioms, and pronunciations. He told me to listen to the radio news on *Voice of America* to improve listening comprehension. He also asked me to write short essays. "Be free to write what comes to your mind. Don't worry. Just write," he said.

A friend, Thiện, told me about the Colombo Plan and that I should apply for a scholarship. "Your English is good. You should take the exam. If you pass, you may get to go to Australia, all expenses paid," he explained. "My brother went to Sydney last year and I hope to go join him." Indeed, the Colombo Plan was a wonderful program offered to kids from war-torn countries to go to college in the British Commonwealth and return to help restore their homelands. The program had been run since the sixties, and it took the best and the brightest from Vietnam if they passed the English test administered by the Australian Embassy in Saigon. I applied.

The day before the test, Titus said, "You will do well. Your listening comprehension is good. Your vocabulary is good. The key is the essay. Remember to write, just write."

The test was hard. I did fine with the multiple-choice questions. I wasn't too confident because I was competing with the best students who had been trained at Hội Việt Mỹ and the finest from all over South Vietnam. I was only a student of the Tin Lành Church. Then came the essay question, "Write a one-page essay about the most interesting person you know."

I stared at the blank page for a while until an idea just came to my mind and I started writing, hesitantly at first and then words just flowed. I wrote about Bình. I wrote about a kid who had no idea what he was going to do—he had no plan, no future. He was a brilliant kid with wild imaginations and dreams, who could accomplish great things had he had the opportunity. I wrote about his losing friendship with me, his best buddy with whom he had shared every meal and every crazy thought. I imagined him in his lonely moments, head in his hands crying. I don't remember how I ended the essay, but time was up and I was drained. I walked out of the exam room exhausted. I knew I missed him, too.

Two weeks later, the list of successful candidates was posted at the Australian Embassy, and I went there with Tài and Thiện to look at it. The names were typed on a sheet of brown paper and pinned on a board, unceremoniously even though it might be the most important and life-changing document for the fifty lives that were chosen to go overseas, all expenses paid. I scanned the list from the top down, somewhere near the end of the page, number 35, was my name. I fixed my eyes there making sure it was me, not even believing what I saw. Could there be someone by the same name? My parents had given me a very unique middle name, so it must be me. Must be. Thiện also passed and I was happy to have a cohort on this adventure.

"Had I competed, I would have won, too," Tài glared. "How come nobody told me about this exam?"

I didn't know why he didn't know about the Colombo Plan. All the kids seemed to know, but he was furious, not at me but the fact that he was left behind.

Now I had to go home and tell Ma. I had never told Ma before that I was taking the test because I thought I would not make it.

Many had tried and failed. I worried how she would feel about my leaving home and going far away for four years.

"Are you sure? Was it really you? Do we have to pay anyone? We don't have any money to send you there. How will you take care of yourself? How long will you be gone? Where is Australia? How will you get there and how will you come back?" She had a million questions and I only had a few answers. I knew that all I could do was to say goodbye to her.

Nobody believed it, even my own Ma. Her son would be a Colombo Plan student, the first in the family to go overseas, the first to go to college. She was proud and sad at the same time. In a couple months, he would leave her and live thousands of miles away. She might not see him for years. He would return when peace was at hand but she didn't know when.

It took her a few days for the news to set in, then she started to make arrangements for my trip. She had a few pairs of pants and shirts made for me. Ma asked me what I wanted before I left Saigon for Sydney, Australia. I said that all I wanted was a meal with a few of my closest friends. She said yes, she would cook us a feast.

Titus was so happy to hear the news. "Well done, my friend. I knew it. You can write," he beamed. Chị Nga invited me to her house for dinner. It was the first time I met her husband, a quiet and grumpy man. He didn't say much and disappeared right after we ate. The girls gave me little gifts to take with me, a small tin box with needles and thread and a card inside: "Thank you, teacher Hao, for the algebra lessons. We can solve problems now. You are a blessed one, teacher Hao. Many people want what you have and you are the chosen one. Remember not to change. We love who you are."

Ma killed two chickens and made a big pot of curry. She served it to my friends with Bánh Mì and rice noodles along with fresh herbs. Tài, Thiện, and Khanh came to enjoy the last feast with me at my house.

"I wish I could go with you. Maybe I will see you there one day," Tài said and gave me a copy of *Ca Khúc Da Vàng* by Trịnh Công Sơn with a message written on the front page:

"A gift to a friend I love best. Dear Hao, I will miss you so much. I will miss our outings, memories for a lifetime. I wish you will always be "Hao" the rest of your life." And he signed it.

Khanh was sad not just for losing me but also for himself. "After you leave, I will be going to training camp. When you come back, I may not be here anymore."

Bình showed up too, although a bit late. He had no gift, but I was glad he came. He was still my best friend.

"Hao, please let's make a promise to each other. No matter where life leads us, let's meet again in front of our school ten years from now. Let's do that for us?" he said, almost crying.

I said yes and we set the date; it would be November 3, 1983, exactly ten years from the day I left Saigon and all my friends there.

Titus wanted one more evening with me and him alone, so I went to his apartment on the top floor of an old building near the Tin Lành Church.

It was a sparse room with a single bed and a desk. Not much else beside a propane cooktop. In the corner was a Martin guitar and a few song books. Titus apologized for his minimalist hospitality.

"Mennonites don't drink, so I have no beer. Let me offer you some juice," he said.

"Why are you here? Why here with us in Vietnam?" I asked a question that I had been longing to ask.

"I hate the war. The killing is pointless. We kill your people and your people kill each other and Americans back home have no idea what's going on and how to end this quagmire. I was drafted, but I am against the war. I volunteered to be a missionary instead. That's my story," he said. "Will you sing me the song about when peace comes?"

I borrowed his guitar and sang the song. "When peace comes, when peace comes," the lyrics repeated itself like a prayer. The idea of peace was alien to me. The war in Vietnam started before I was born—when the French bowed out and Americans weighed in. I was ten years old when the bombs started to fall on our land. I was thirteen when I saw death in the streets of Saigon. Every day, someone I knew got killed. *When peace comes? Will it ever come?* I choked up.

"Let me sing you my favorite song. This is about me, far away from Ohio, being here in Vietnam with you." He took back the Martin to play this song. His voice was warm and rich, his eyes wet.

> *If you miss the train I'm on*
> *You will know that I am gone*
> *You can hear the whistle blow*
> *A hundred miles…A hundred miles…A hundred miles*

When he finished, both of us sat silent. I knew he missed Ohio and would rather be there than in Saigon. He sought comfort in people like me whom he could somehow help. I didn't realize then that later his song would become mine, not a hundred miles, not even five hundred, but a continent, an ocean, and a world away.

Mango Death

One more time, I returned to Vietnam, but this time for a sad trip. I came to pay my respects to my younger brother's wife. She died a sudden and mysterious death. She was in her early forties, a robust farmer most of her life. For one year, she had fevers and headaches. Her skin turned yellow and she gained weight, mostly water. Hospitals in the small towns could not diagnose her symptoms. Doctors tried different medications, hoping something might work. My brother Hòa worried a lot, but his wife Phương insisted that it was nothing. She braved the pain and continued to manage the mango farm—their pride and joy—until she died.

The taxi driver dropped me off at the farm, and I gave him a good tip for driving slowly and keeping a decent safety distance of a few feet from the big trucks. It was a difficult job to drive in Vietnam and I could not even think of doing that myself. Every inch of the road was filled with rumbling trucks loaded with merchandise, private vehicles with blacked out windows and motorcycles carrying a family of four, not to mention people and their baskets crossing the road. I had told him beforehand I didn't care about the time. As long as he didn't hit anyone or even the chicken crossing the road, I would be pleased. I thanked him and told him to come back for me three days later.

A couple of raggedy dogs barked and bared their fangs. "Quiet!" My brother Hòa stumbled out from behind the farmhouse. He was a tall and lean man with dark tanned skin and sun-bleached hair. He had a crooked smile that looked more like a grimace. He put his long arm around my shoulders and led me to the stone table under the big mango tree. He poured me a cup of tea and offered me a cigarette. I seldom smoked, but here at the farm with my brothers, I made an exception.

"Brother Xê, welcome back to Tay Ninh. How was the trip?"

I told him about the traffic, which was worse every time I returned.

"Business is booming. These trucks cross into Cambodia through here. We have many accidents, the highest rate in the nation." He frowned, looking at the main road in front of the farmhouse. Trucks, vans, ox carts full of sugarcane passed by in the heat of midday.

"Please make yourself at home, take a siesta—the hammock there is for you." He offered. There wasn't much to do so I followed his advice and napped for a couple of hours straight.

"I am tired of this mango business," my brother Hòa said later after dinner. "We were a team, Phương and I. We built this farm together from nothing. This is the land that nobody wanted. What you see here is twenty years of labor, hers and mine."

I saw that. They had built forty acres of mango trees. They started out with one acre of forested land the government gave to each family of settlers. They cut down trees, grew cashew, sweet potatoes, coconuts, and worked with fellow villagers to dig a canal to bring in water. They experimented with different crops and fruit trees, and finally, mango became their success story. Hòa is the youngest of my brothers, only ten years old when my mother and my brothers arrived here in the New-Economic Zone of Tay Ninh, a few kilometers from the Cambodian border.

"You would not believe what was here before," my brother said. "During the war, this area was a jungle of huge trees, one meter or so in diameter. Sometimes this land belonged to the Khmer, sometimes to Vietnam. They killed us, we killed them, but the forest kept us separate."

"The Government told us to clear the land, cut down the trees and grow cassava. It was such a waste. The trees were large and old. You are talking about ebony, mahogany, teak! We sawed them down and burned them because we couldn't haul them anywhere with our bare hands. The forest burned for weeks. The ash was ankle deep. My eyes were swollen shut and oozing with pus. My lungs burned with hot smoke."

I had met Phương at the farm on my first trip home after twenty years of living overseas. She greeted me with a broad smile on a freckled face without make-up. Her skin was brown and smooth like polished wood. Her long black hair was shiny and tied back with a simple hair clip.

"Anh Xê!" She cried the same greeting every time I saw her. She called me by my nickname: Brother C for number three in the series of seven sons. She led me down the dirt path to the thatch-roofed house that they had built with local timber and bamboo. Her long black hair swept gently against her slim, muscular back as her arms swung wide the way peasants walk.

"Anh Xê, welcome to Tay Ninh," she greeted me in her sing-song voice. "Please come stay with us as often as you want, as long as you can. We don't have much here, but we have heart. You are always part of the family even though you live so far away."

I loved her voice—a blend of an austere northern accent she inherited from her parents and the easy-going way of the Mekong Delta. People came to this village from all walks of life, and the local accent was born of the mix—a bit of everything baked together by the hot sun of the Tay Ninh border town.

"I love the farm life, the simple life that I don't have in America. I love it here," I groaned with pleasure leaning back in a hammock. Life on the farm is basic. It is all about food—growing it, cooking it, selling it. It certainly was easy for me to say. I was on vacation and had no idea about the hard work of the farmers.

Phương headed out to the yard with a rusty machete to fetch firewood. Under an old straw hat in midday sun, she squatted and whacked a dry cashew branch to forearm-length pieces. Her thin arm raised and chopped a few times before the dry wood broke. She gathered the sticks and headed to the sooty kitchen behind the house. She giggled as she saw me watch her work, "Anh Xê, you should take an afternoon nap. Everyone here does that in this heat."

"I don't take naps—not what we do in America," I said.

"Anh Xê, you are an educated person. You must have seen so many countries and cities. What is it like out there?" She looked at me with her eyebrows raised.

"It is big and lonely. I have a good job, a nice house, and a car." I didn't know what else to say.

"The women must be lovely. I have seen them on TV—blond hair, blue eyes, tall, and they always have beautiful white teeth," she wiped the sweat off her forehead, with a sigh.

"That's just TV. Most people I know are not like that. They eat; they sleep; they use the toilet."

She laughed.

"I grew up here, you know? I was a little girl when my family came here. I can barely read or write. Anh Hòa and I have been married eight years now and we are a good team. The kids are healthy. We have gone hungry for a long time—we have done so many things just to survive—we are going to make it here, you will see."

Hòa and Phương made great improvements to the farm over the years. Every time I visited they had added something new. The first year, they acquired an old Massey Ferguson tractor left over from the days of President Diem's rural development campaign. It was a rusty red machine as massive as a water buffalo and worked just as hard although a water buffalo would not break down or need spare parts as often. The neighbors paid Hòa to plow their fields, and that money was enough to fix the truck and subsidize farm expenses. The following years, Hòa purchased the neighbors' lots when many of them quit the farm life and went back to the city where they could work in the shade.

Hòa had also cut down the cashew trees and experimented with new crops. "Why cashew in the first place?" I asked.

"They are care free," Hòa explained. "They gave us shade, fruit, and nuts, and we didn't have to do anything. They didn't need much water or fertilizer. The nuts are worth a few dollars a kilo."

Phương used to soak the cashew nuts in a bucket of water so they weighed more. She giggled when she explained it to me, "Everybody does it and they all know the trick. We do it anyway."

After cashew, they planted cassava because it was easy to grow and the demand was high. "You stick cuttings in the ground, leave them alone, and except for a bit of weeding, then you get a ton or so per hectare. The weeds we'd sell to cow farmers; the cassava roots we'd eat or sell to merchants to make tapioca and monosodium glutamate. The problem is you can't control the price. Too many people doing the same, and the crop's worthless!"

I also witnessed the beginning of a mango farm. The only mango tree on the farm at the time was the one my mother planted when the family first got there, before there was a house, before there was enough to eat. She grew it from a flat seed the size of a baby's hand and it grew so large its shade covered the entire house.

"Look at the future!" Hòa pointed out to me the many mango saplings in canvas sacs of soil and root balls. "These are grafted mango trees from Cambodia. They grow best in the dry heat of the Tay Ninh area. They are very sweet and expensive. Imagine a few years from now, we will sit back and watch the money roll in." He smiled, puffing on a Craven cigarette.

Sure enough, whenever I returned to the farm years later, I told the taxi driver to drop me off at Mr. Hòa's mango farm in Tay Ninh and they knew exactly where to go. The locals knew the mango farm as a landmark, a model of success, a miracle of modernization in a place where nobody thought it was possible to make a living. Next to the canal that channels water from the west to the village is an expanse of mango trees, forty acres of green leaves and mangos dangling on long stalks.

"Anh Xê!" Phương ran out to greet me with the same bright smile. "Please come in. How was your trip? The road is better now, we have electricity. We even cook with gas!"

The farm was beautiful! The mango trees had grown tall and thick and they formed a solid canopy across many acres around the farmhouse. Their glossy long leaves provided shades over strings of mango the size of my fist and hanging from these long stalks. My brother Hòa and his wife had made it happen. The house had been rebuilt with bricks and blocks and the driveway was covered with gravel so trucks could back in.

Before Tết and near the end of the dry season, mangos were selling like live shrimp, as the saying goes. Trucks came from Saigon to load up large baskets of perfect mangos. Dealers paid in advance before the fruits grew large, betting that all those flowers would stick around and turn into money for both the farmer and the retailers.

Phương hovered over a dozen "troops" with the picking, sorting, and packing. Hòa supervised the weighing and loading to make sure nobody stole or cheated. Night fell and they had time to spend with me. We sat down to eat under the large mango tree. The meal was far more elaborate this time than ever before, complete with spring rolls, roast chicken, vermicelli and fresh herbs. Hòa even bought Heineken instead of the cheap old Saigon beer that he used to serve with ice.

"Anh Xê! Did you see the new fish pond we put in?" She sang these words as she told me about new projects on the farm. "We put in many baby carp, but we were too busy taking care of the mango trees, and the fish all died." I thought it was odd that the fish died because carp can take just about anything.

After my mother died, I didn't find the need to make the long trek home as often as I did before. I got news that the farm kept improving and the income from mango could not be beat. Twenty or thirty thousand dollars a year was a large sum of money to be made in Vietnam and Hòa and Phương were becoming rich and famous.

Then came the shocking news. It is a mystery how she died. I only know she died suddenly and what killed her was never clear.

They said she died of blood poisoning and she should have had blood transfusions to save her life. Some said it was a brain disease, an inflammation of some sort, or an amoeba infection that finally got her. Nobody really knew and the doctors in Vietnam said that had she been treated sooner, they could have saved her life. They wanted money, up front, lots of it, but it was too little too late. She had a fever, lost consciousness, lapsed into a coma and died.

It took me weeks to obtain a tourist visa to return to Vietnam, and I couldn't attend her funeral. I went to Phương's grave to pay my belated respects. I insisted on walking the mile in the heat to the graveyard where my mother also rested. Nobody in the village even walked anymore—they all rode motorcycles the way Americans drive cars. I preferred to walk around the farmhouse and explore the village. I could think clearly and see the little dirt trails and the farm life away from the main road that had become a busy one-lane highway.

I walked along the canal between the cassava fields and the young rubber tree plantation. In the glowing afternoon sun, I saw the graveyard marked by a cross behind the Catholic Church. Phương's grave was a few rows in front of my mother's, both built with bricks and cement the shape of a raised coffin, covered with blue tiles and a gray granite slab. Encased in the smooth stone, the latest picture of Phương stared back at me. The picture was taken when she had already been sick, and she didn't look like the farm girl I used to know. In the picture, she had already gained some weight and looked more like a farm boss with stern downcast eyes. She didn't smile with her straight teeth and a few crow's feet around the jet-black eyes. The cemetery was eerily quiet. There was no sing-song voice to tell me stories about her life as a young farm girl walking through the fields and smelling sweet new rice. I didn't hear her quizzing me about my traveling life that she thought was beyond her dreams. From the stone, a serious looking woman in a yellow *Áo Dài* frowned—not the broad smile and the buoyant "Anh Xê!" greeting that I came to expect. I wished I could cry, but no tears came despite the incense smoke in my eyes.

"Something isn't right," Hòa said when we sat down together later in the evening beneath the old mango tree. "We went to Saigon to take our daughter to college. It was supposed to be a quick trip, in and out, nothing special."

"Before we went, Phương had a fever, but she had been having fevers. She took a few aspirins and ignored them. She was a tough woman and never complained about anything. Never."

"Then the day we got to Saigon, she ran a high fever and collapsed. She could not remember her name, my name, our daughter's name. I rushed her to the hospital where she rested for a day. Her memory came back and I was so happy but that didn't last long. She lapsed in and out of consciousness. The doctors all said they knew the problem, but every one of them had a different opinion. Who was I to believe?" Hòa's eyes watered and I placed a hand on his shoulder.

"Brother Hòa, you know how much I love you, how much I love Phương, how much I love this place. I love to come home to this place, whenever I can. I am so sorry."

"Anh Xê, you know we had no choice. You are an educated man and you have choices. We grew up here and this is the world we know and it is the world we built. We did the best we could and the best we did could have killed Phương."

I had a sense of what Hòa was saying but who am I to say what is right or wrong for anyone? We all did the best we could. Hòa pointed out to me with a broad sweep of his hand, "Look at this farm, it is beautiful, isn't it? But Phương is not here. She is gone."

"Do you know what was wrong with her?" I had to ask even though I was afraid of the answer.

"Do you know how tough it is to be a mango farmer? Unlike other people in the city, we only get paid once a year, when we sell the fruits. It is a gamble. If we don't have mangos to sell, we lose. If the fruits come out at the wrong time, we lose it all. If we don't get paid for the investment, we lose a year and sometimes two or three. That's why we need to spray."

He told me about the hormones he used to trigger the flowering of the mango, plus the insecticides and fertilizers. He experimented with them all so that he could time his own production to beat the market. Mango is the king of all tropical fruits, and sometimes off-season is the best way to make money.

The rusty old Massey Ferguson rested under a tin roof, retired for good. Next to the shed lay a few of Hòa's proudest inventions: the stainless steel fifty-gallon tanks mounted on wheels and connected to gas-powered pumps. Hoses and accessories scattered about next to a pile of empty plastic bottles of insecticides, fungicides, and herbicides made in the USA, Canada, Japan, and mostly unlabeled from China.

"You see? If you don't spray, the flowers will drop prematurely and there is no fruit, the bugs will eat the mangos and nobody buys them, the weeds will choke out the trees, and we can't make money. We can't go back to the old days when we had nothing and had to grow cassava for pennies. We can't."

In silence, we sat smoking cigarettes thinking about Phương. I didn't know what was turning in Hòa's mind but in mine, Phương smiled brightly and called out "Anh Xê!" I finally cried.

Ghosts

"Remember me?"

The tired, sad voice on the phone reminded me of a teenager whose voice had just dropped one octave. I had not heard his voice for thirty years. I froze. What can you say to a ghost?

"Do you know how long I have been looking for you?" his voice shook like the bass string of a guitar. I trembled—like a debt collector had caught up with me.

In Vietnam, we'd burn incense and put food on the altars for the ghosts. We dropped paper money in the alms box at the local pagoda and asked the monks to pray for their lost souls so that they would find peace.

"Bình! Where the hell are you? I've been looking for you for years. How did you find me?"

"I live in Houston. Been here for a while. Come see me, okay?"

"Okay."

So, I flew to Houston for a long weekend to see Bình. I was going to meet with a living ghost. For a long time, I had given him up for dead. I had always assumed that he would not survive the fall of Saigon and the years after Giải Phóng.

I found him waiting for me at the baggage area of George Bush International Airport. He stood still like a blue heron in a stream of moving travelers. He had a very steady stance due to poor eyesight. Practically blind due to nearsightedness, he moved with extreme efficiency—but only when he could see.

He wore a few new scars on a face dotted with age spots like a ripened banana, and a perpetual frown. The biggest scar was on his right forehead as if someone had whacked him with a two by four. Long, oily black hair framed his face. He combed it back like Antonio Banderas. His body slouched over a bit, but he still carried a strong and sturdy frame beneath a worn black denim field coat. As long as I had known him, he was never a sharp dresser like some other friends. He preferred the tough look. I could still see the broad-shouldered wrestler in him whom I would hate to mess with. Since our childhood, I have always been the poet, and he the general. He has no fear of pain or death, while I agonize over everything and everyone.

When we hugged—longer than socially acceptable—I smelled cigarette smoke on his breath and oily hair. He had a little trouble recognizing me as I had changed far more: Three decades of good living made me well-padded and bald.

"I still recognize your smile, Hao. People change but something about them doesn't change," he gripped my shoulders with both hands.

We sat in the quiet of our own thoughts as Bình drove from the airport to his house in a suburb of Houston. Despite his eyesight, he could drive his truck just fine, though he confessed, "I can only drive in bright daylight."

We arrived at his house in the suburb, a one-story rambler with faded green wood siding surrounded by trees and a big yard. A shallow gutter ran along the sidewalk to drain flood water when it rained hard in Houston. Outside in the garden stood a few banana trees. Pink and white bougainvillea flowers framed the garage. Scattered everywhere were pots of mint, lemongrass and other Vietnamese herbs. Inside his house was dark and musty, the humidity and stale cigarette smoke mixed with Vietnamese fish sauce.

"My wife just packed up and left," he waved his hand at the cluttered house. "She isn't happy with me. I don't make much money and she likes shopping." He didn't show any regrets—he hadn't changed a bit.

After showing me the couch where I would make myself at home, he went into the kitchen to look for a bottle of wine and some snacks in the fridge.

"You are always the good guy, Hao." He cleared the coffee table of a few dirty dishes and a big mug he used as an ashtray. "Your mother gave you that smile and it has helped you through life. You are very lucky." Indeed, I have a quick smile and an easy laugh, which makes people expect that I'll take care of things. Bình's always been irresponsible, so people just shrug, expect nothing from him and say that's typical because he is Bình.

"I have my problems too, you know?"

Bình broke open the bottle of cheap Merlot and offered me a cigarette. "You're still the good boy," he snapped when I turned down the smoke. We drank and chewed soy sauce chicken. Salty meat and cheap Merlot somehow worked well together.

"What are you doing now?" I finally asked.

"Let me show you." Bình took an old classical guitar from a beat-up black case. The spruce top had aged into a bleached white patina and its pock-marked varnish matched the mottled skin of the owner.

"You, the musician? Never."

"We all changed, you know? What happened to the little boy who had nothing? What happened to your hair? You are a fat cat now," he teased.

Bình struck a tuning fork on the edge of the coffee table and held the buzzing tongs to his right ear. He joked as he adjusted the nylon strings, "Do you know this tune? Mi-Mi, Si-Si, Sol-Sol, Re-Re, La-La, Mi-Mi." Then he took a deep breath and bent his head over the guitar's upper bout stuck firmly in his chest.

He hugged the instrument for almost a minute and slowly lifted his hands to play. The shape of his hands had not changed: rough and large-boned but now heavily scarred. He played the simple "Romanza" that every student of the classical guitar learns first. Notes floated out of the sound hole as his right fingers plucked the strings—each note rang clear and vibrated with colors. The traditional Spanish melody floated above the arpeggios and the heavy beats of the bass notes. The song in E minor was sweet and sad and a bit sunnier when it turned to E major in the middle before it came back to minor again, ending with a few descending notes like a sigh. He returned the guitar to its case and lit another cigarette. I left him with his thoughts for a minute.

"I never thought you had any musical bone in your body. I thought you might be a judo teacher at best, but a musician. What the hell happened to you?"

"What happened to us? What happened to the whole country? To all of us?" he choked out. "Remember Khanh? The poor bastard. Barely eighteen. Oldest son of nine. He took care of his mother and the younger kids. He had no time to study. You remember the cassava cake business that he started?" he asked.

"Yes, Khanh fed his whole family selling cassava cake." I loved that sweet ground-up cassava and coconut mixed with sugar and condensed milk baked to a golden brown. "He sold that in front of our school and the girls' school from the back of his bicycle."

"Right after you left, he flunked the college entrance exams and went in; six months of boot camp; three months in the jungle. Someone shot him in the kidney while he was taking a leak in the middle of the night. Maybe the VC shot him, maybe not." Bình lit another cigarette, "Took him six hours to die. Must have hurt like hell. Just think about looking at your own bloody guts poured out on the jungle floor. The poor bastard. He was barely an adult. He never had a girl, never felt a breast, let alone being inside a woman."

Khanh still haunts me. I have a faded photo of him taken as a cadet, barely five feet tall and at best one hundred pounds. A few months of training and then he was sent to the central highlands. In combat uniform and the heavy steel helmet, he looked like a smiling mushroom. His death sentence was almost certain like with so many young men. When I heard he died, I sent his family my savings—about twenty dollars. It paid for the funeral meal.

"You were mad at me for being me," Bình continued. "You were always the good student. I didn't give a shit. You left Saigon with a scholarship. I didn't have a clue what to do. Hell, nobody else did."

"I was not mad at you," I said. "I was worried about you. You could have ended up like Khanh."

"Do you believe in ghosts?" he asked.

"No, I've never seen one. Okay, I used to be afraid of the dark and being alone but I have learned to live alone for a long time. Darkness doesn't bother me either."

"You are lucky. I have seen many. I live with them." He pointed at the altar and the incense sticks smoldering in his backyard among the banana plants.

"I was in the jungle, thick with mosquitoes and leeches. After Giải Phóng, I was forced to join the youth volunteer army. I had a mission in Cambodia to bring back dead bodies. The war back home was over, but the war with the Khmer continued on. We killed them, they killed us. They killed their own people too." Bình waved his cigarette as his frown deepened.

"One night, I was looking for a place to sleep. I was tired and hungry and separated from the team. Usually, I slept in a hammock or on a tarp but it rained so hard, there was no place to stay dry. I saw a small hut in the trees and headed to it. I hoped to ask the owner to let me sit in a corner for the night. The hut was in bad shape but at least it could shelter a hunter overnight. "Anybody home?" I asked. Nobody answered. I pressed on the door and it creaked open. In the dark I saw a few planks of wood, enough for a small bed. Nothing else was around as signs of recent occupants. I let myself in and crashed on the floor."

"Something woke me up, not a sound but a sight. In the doorway, a skinny figure stood motionless. He must have been watching me for a long time. Must be the hunter returning to find his hut invaded. I uttered a few words of apology: 'Forgive me. I was tired. I found nobody home.' He was silent. Not a word. Not any movement. I sat up, my back against the wall. We stared at each other—it seemed like a long time. Then in a fraction of a second, he was next to me with his hands stretched out for my face. I reacted with judo reflexes to deflect. I felt for the elbows. He was too quick for me and kept me from getting a grip. Finally, I found his bony wrist and applied an arm lock. His arm loosened like a rope as I twisted it: No joints! I took a look at his face in the dim light through the doorway: No face! I was so scared I bolted out the door and ran for the river. I ran and ran, and till my legs gave out, and I collapsed in the mud."

I looked at Bình's face for any sign that he was making up stuff. He usually cracked a brief smile. Sometimes he'd just guffaw when I fell for it. I know him well for the gift of storytelling and bravado. He was closer to me than my own brothers when we grew up together in Saigon. We spent seven years in the same classrooms, hung out after school to get into mischief, sharing every morsel of good food.

"How is your arm?" he teased.

"It's okay, a bit crooked, but okay. I can't play tennis worth a damn because I can't toss the ball straight up in the air. Other than that, I have no complaints. I continued judo though. I took it up again in college, and broke my front teeth. Started again in my thirties, got a brown belt and then broke my neck. I decided to quit after an expensive surgery to fuse the cervical C5-C6," I said.

"Geez. Bad karma. I should never have introduced you to that sport. You are just no good at it."

In high school, we were judo buddies. We often ate at each other's houses, and our mothers treated us like brothers. When we had a bit of money for Tết, we would go out for a bowl of *Phở*. When we didn't have enough, we would split a *Bánh Mì* in half. We studied together, went home together with arms around each other's shoulders. We sometimes took a siesta in each other's bed. No big deal. In the U.S., it would have been taken a different way, but in Vietnam, there was no stigma.

Even at the age of eleven, Bình had already developed muscular arms and chest from doing push-ups and chin-ups. He looked really cool with the threadbare judo suit rolled up inside a cotton laundry bag slung over his shoulder. We spent the morning hours at the Saigon dojo run by Buddhist monks who had trained at the Kodokan in Japan. Back in 1962 many of them got mowed down in the streets with real bullets for demonstrating against President Diem's oppression. Since then, it seemed the survivors stuck to teaching and quit political activities.

I loved everything about judo—the Gentle Way—the idea that the bamboo bends but doesn't break. The *tatami* mats smelled musty with sweat and blood. Black belt monks moved like gentle giants among dozens of kids in white suits and different belt colors: white, yellow, orange, green, blue, brown, and a few black. Children's laughter and the loud slamming on mats woke up a few city blocks. After practice, we sat on our heels for five minutes like straight rows of little monks to meditate. The teachers walked around with long wooden paddles and gently whacked the kids who didn't focus.

Of the sixty-four throwing techniques in the Kodokan repertoire, *seoi nage* is clearly the most elegant. *Seoi* also means "sweet rice" in Vietnamese, and we had much of it for breakfast. Our monk teacher prescribed 20 *seois* as punishment for everything: tardiness, not sitting straight in meditation, whatever. One day, we came to class late and received our *seoi* penalty.

I was dreaming of a hot bowl of noodle soup when Bình dropped me over his shoulder. Four months of practice was not enough time to drill the *ukemi*—the technique for proper falling— into my reflexes. Instead of slamming my entire arm against the mat to break the fall, I stuck my hand out. Next, I felt a sharp pain, and when I looked: my left arm had three joints, and my fingers could touch the elbow. All the kids gathered around while I lay on the mat, trying not to wail. I was more worried about explaining the broken arm to my mother than the pain itself. My teacher patched me up with a couple of splints and a makeshift sling and sent me home with some vitamin pills.

How could things go wrong so quickly? How could pure joy turn to pain in a fraction of time? Worse yet, my mother cried when she saw me come home with a bandaged arm. For many weeks she didn't let me go out with Bình and stopped giving him treats when he came over. From then on, she just considered him a bad influence.

My mother was right: Bình was a bad influence—but one that I needed. We spent most of our time together the way he wanted to spend it—with girls. He developed a way of talking to them that made them fall in love with him. The women's boyfriends picked fights with us. Most of the time, he did the heavy fighting while I watched his back. The other boys used chains, knives, and pipes as weapons. Bình acted like he could throw anybody over the fence and somehow, his bravado worked. We never got beat up.

He was the reason I met Trang. While everyone in school already boasted about a girlfriend, I didn't have any. My reputation as *nhát gái* (girl-shy) had begun to bother Bình. "I have to find you a nice girl," he said. I don't know how he did it but after a little time, he told me about a girl who needed tutoring. "She is not pretty but she is a daughter of an officer, just like your father. Be careful around her, her father may shoot you."

"Don't worry. I will teach her."

So twice a week, I went to Trang's house. We sat across the table and she would read the text from *English for Today*. I corrected her pronunciation to make sure it was textbook correct. She was studious just like me, but we didn't talk much and she didn't smile either. Throughout six months or so of tutoring, I never had the urge to reach across the table for her hand. I didn't ask her out for a date, nor did I even know what to do if we actually went out on a date. Nothing happened. I was not in love with her.

All my friends, especially Bình, were way ahead of me in the love department. I wasn't sure if any of their bragging stories were true, but they sure were prolific. I only knew for sure of Bình's stories because I saw him in action. Bình hit on street vendors, older women whose husbands were away at war, prostitutes even.

In our all-boys school, we fantasized about Miss Liên, our favorite teacher who lactated through her white Áo Dài and wiggled as she wrote on the blackboard. She was the best. As Miss Liên was the subject of our lust, Linh was the woman we worshiped. She was our schoolmaster's daughter, who came by now and then from the girls' school. She floated across the schoolyard in a white Áo Dài, her long black hair flowing down her back like a silk cascade. All the boys got excited every time she was spotted in the vicinity and buzzed like drones. She was a pure goddess in the dust and noise of Saigon. No boy had the nerve to touch her, not even Bình.

One day, I happened to be a few steps behind Linh—and the fluidness of her long black hair and white dress floating in the warm air. She sensed my presence, paused, but never turned around. I wouldn't know what to say if she did. A gust of wind came up and she held onto the long white flaps of her dress. I had never seen softer or longer fingers and for just those few seconds, I fell in love with her hands. Another day I happened to turn the corner and she was right in front of me. She lowered her eyes and stepped to the side waiting for me to pass. I froze. She smiled and when she walked past me as I caught the fragrance of the plumeria flower in her hair.

"Take a nap, you must be tired from the trip." Bình let me lie down on the couch while he went to the garage to work on his projects. He loved audio equipment and built custom-made speakers, special orders, and hand finished them with French polish.

"Let's go out for Phở tonight, for old times' sake," I suggested before dozing off.

The Vietnamese neighborhood in Houston was vibrant with restaurants and nail salons. Texas had attracted many refugees with more affordable housing and warm climates, unlike many Midwest and the Northern states I have lived in. We walked into the Saigon 75 restaurant and found a corner table. Many restaurants are named Saigon followed by a number to differentiate them and bring back memories of how the owners came to America. Number 75, 80, and sometimes 85 marked the year they came to America. Some are named after famous streets of Saigon, too. The bowls were large—three times the portions that we used to have back home. We talked about the days when Saigon fell and what happened to him.

"Then came April 1975. Damn! You had already left. What a fucking mess!" Bình said. "President Thieu fled the country a month ahead. The generals took off in stolen military airplanes and navy ships with their families, weeks before the VC arrived in Saigon. We hardly put up a fight, not like we did at the Tết Offensive in 1968. The leadership had left with their gold and suitcases full of dollars. They just left."

I remembered watching the fall of Saigon from afar while I was a new student in Canberra. News came in day by day: Quang

Tri fell, then Da Nang, Ban Me Thuot, city by city. Without leadership, soldiers dropped their weapons, stripped away their uniforms and ran home to take care of their families. Like a machete splitting a sugar cane, the North came straight down to Saigon without any resistance--they were surprised themselves that taking over the South was so easy. It was nothing like Tết 68.

"I wandered around the streets, not sure what to do. Should I fight? Should I go home?" Bình put down his chopsticks and stared at me. "Should I head to the American embassy? They wouldn't let me in anyway because I had no papers. I loved Vietnam and didn't want to leave, but I knew it would never be the same. Not for me. Not for people like us on the losing side of the war."

"Tell me about those years after '75. What did you do to survive?" I asked.

"I shared a street corner with another guy. We owned an old cyclo. At least I could make money selling my labor. Do you remember those old three-wheel cyclos? The customers sit in front, and the driver leans on the pedals in the back with all his weight. Have you ever pushed a cyclo in the heat? Even as strong as I was, I couldn't push it uphill. My buddy worked half the day while I slept and I took over the cyclo when he slept. One day I was so tired and overslept. I woke up and the cyclo was gone along with my buddy."

"Nice guy!" I said.

"I volunteered to go to Cambodia for two years to fight the Pol Pot army. That was the only choice for many people our age. We were to redeem our fathers' sins against the regime with our free labor. They gave us each a poncho, a pair of boots, a canteen and our job was to carry equipment for the troops. We were not allowed to touch any weapons no matter what, even when we were shot at. Cambodia in the rainy season became the muddiest place on earth. There was no place to camp. We placed the ponchos down and slept in them until we sank in the mud. Then we moved a few feet and spread out again trying to keep dry. Sometimes the mortar rounds came down on us, and there was no place to hide. We sat there in the dark waiting for the shelling to stop so we could then pick up the bodies to ship home.

"After I came home, I learned to make guitars with the guys in Nguyễn Thiện Thuật Street who made and sold musical instruments. We made guitars from scrap wood and broken furniture. They were terrible compared to the Yamahas but they played. But strings we couldn't find. We used fishing lines, steel wires, and copper wires from old transformers. Some of the guys were classically trained at the Conservatory of Music before the fall of Saigon and now they lived in the streets too. One taught me Romanza and I fell in love with the sound. I can't see much, but I can hear. I learned to play a few pieces and made money playing at bus stops and restaurants. We were all hungry so we stuck together. When I came to America, music was the only skill I had, so I taught guitar to inner city kids in Houston and played nightclubs for a living. I make do, you know?"

"I asked around for news about you, but nobody knew. My mother said you went to Cambodia and then she never heard from you again. I thought you were dead so I stopped looking," I said.

Back at the house, Bình found another bottle of Merlot. "Don't you believe in ghosts?" He wanted to be sure.

Vietnamese literature is filled with ghost stories: ghosts of the jungle, the streets, the corner of the house, and the rafters. They lurk everywhere. Some appear as beautiful maidens to lure you to their beds and then swallow your souls. You learn to be afraid of the dark, alone.

On one of my trips back to Vietnam, I toured Cat Tien National Park with a few of my Forest Service colleagues. We were there to help Professor Kiet and local ecologists with management plans, the American way. I was driving with them in the dark after a long day walking through the bamboo jungle looking for signs of the rare Javan rhinos that had been captured by infrared camera. Ahead of the car in the high beams, pairs of glowing red eyes danced in the night, just like the ghost stories I read in my childhood. "Night jars," Dr. Kiet explained. "Their dilated eyes reflect light just like that." I supposed that's what people saw as ghosts of the jungle. The banyan tree roots in moonlight could be so eerie, just like floating headless ghosts.

I shook my head, and Bình looked up at me, his eyes narrow: "I believe that ghosts roam Cambodia. So many souls wander around trying to find their way home. Imagine young girls and boys...I can never forget what they did to my comrades. There were ghosts everywhere I turned. They grabbed my arms and legs when I fell asleep. I am near blind but I know what I saw. I arranged bodies in a wooden boat to take them home—heads pointed to the front, legs to the back. Overnight, half of them turned one way, half the other. I burned plenty of incense to appease the ghosts and finally, they didn't bother me again."

Bình filled my empty glass, "I have talked enough. Tell me about you and all the years you were overseas. What the hell happened to your hair?"

"You know, I had it good," I confessed. "I never went hungry. I never got shot at. I worked hard, but who didn't? I must have tried every job: washing dishes in restaurants, mowing grass, cleaning toilets, driving forklifts, delivering pizzas, you name it. First job in a restaurant, I was a little slow and the boss yelled at me: 'Either you work with both hands or you don't work here.' I worked faster and she left me alone. I sent all my savings home to my mother and brothers. I wish I could have done more. I wish I could have helped you. I missed everything about Vietnam. I almost went crazy the first few months thinking about my mother, my home, you guys, everyone there. I even missed the smelly fish sauce. The refugees didn't come here until 1975 so there were no Vietnamese restaurants before that at all. There was no grocery, fish sauce, rice, nothing."

"Hey! Cheer up. You know who else I found?" He humored me. "Remember Trang, your student? She lives in Houston. Do you want to meet her?"

"Sure. I wonder how she is doing."

"A husband and a couple of kids. Typical family. No drama like me."

"Maybe best I leave her alone."

"Remember Linh? Do you know what happened to her? All our friends are still looking for her after all these years." I had to ask. Bình sighed.

"I saved enough to buy a place in one of the escape schemes. Linh was among the people on my boat. The going price was one ounce of gold apiece. Each boat packed in a few hundred people. They used these wooden boats to ship pigs and cattle up and down the Mekong. In the 80's, they packed the hulls with refugees. The boat stank of animals—and fear, sweat, sick bodies, urine, shit. Linh was with her father, only a few spaces from me. Out in the ocean, pirates rammed us. I thought our old wooden boat would break apart and sink with us in it. They came on board with their AK-47's shouting and shooting. We stayed down while they robbed us. They pulled away the women and young girls. The women had prepared for this by shaving their hair and spreading engine grease all over their bodies. That didn't stop the pirates. They came for Linh. I stood up and they slammed something to the side of my head. I passed out for hours and woke up with a bloody face. The girls never came back the same. Some jumped in the ocean and drowned. People threw pieces of foam and wood for them to grab but they just floated away. Linh didn't come back and I never saw her again. Promise me to tell nobody. I want us all to remember her the way she was." He rubbed the scar on his forehead.

His words crushed the air out of my lungs.

"Let me play you my favorite song," Bình said. He cradled the guitar and immersed himself again in the sounds that came from under his hands. The music started out slowly as a dark melody and it quickened with dissonance. The middle part turned to a bright sunny major, then dropped suddenly back to mellow melancholy. Then anger and pain poured out from my friend's broken fingertips as he eased the melody into a haunting coda that left me exhausted.

"You know? I love Villa-Lobos," slowly, Bình put the guitar away. "He wrote this prelude for his wife, but for me, it's about struggle: light and darkness, kindness versus cruelty. Evil and darkness always wins. I know it and you know it."

He lit me a cigarette. I took a drag out of friendship.

"In 1983, you had already been gone for ten years. Saigon fell soon after you left," he continued. "I went to our school and sat in front of the gate waiting for you. November 3rd, right? That was the day we said goodbye. Remember our pact? We promised to see each other in front of our school after ten years? No matter what? I sat there the whole day thinking about all our friends, you the most. I knew that you would not show up. But I was there, as we promised."

"Let us meet again in ten years in front of the gate, no matter what," Bình had made me swear the night before I left Saigon for college in Australia. He cut his hand with a knife and I did the same. My bloody hand touched his to seal our promise, the one I couldn't keep.

"The day we were supposed to meet again, I was still a new immigrant in America, a struggling student, washing dishes in restaurants to pay rent. I couldn't go home because I had become a refugee, an exile, not allowed back. It took me twenty years to get back home. By then everything had changed and I could not find you. I didn't forget the pact. I just could not come home." I choked up.

"Hey, my friend, drink up." He flashed a crooked smile and clinked his glass of Merlot with mine. "Don't be sad. I found you, didn't I? And I will never lose you again!"

The Ocean

I wanted to be a merchant marine, to sail the Pacific and Indian oceans and captain a ship—to visit all the cities along the coast of Vietnam, drop into Hong Kong harbor, the islands of Japan and the Philippines, Singapore, and one day south to Australia.

The ocean was my first love. It was how I felt about the girl next door when I was thirteen. I didn't even know her name, and I didn't know how to ask. I saw her now and then in her white *Áo Dài* when she was going out or coming back from school. Her long black hair cascaded down the slender curve of her back. I knew that she knew I was there, but she only threw a sideways glance. I believed she could make me very happy. I could drown in her watery eyes and would not survive.

It was Uncle Đúng who got me hooked when I turned seventeen. He took me on a short trip, three days from Saigon to Da Nang aboard the *Trường Hải*, the ship on which he served as the chief engineer. The *Trường Hải* was no luxury cruise ship. It was bulky, greasy, and coated in layers of gray and black paint. It constantly rocked with the waves and roared with the deafening Mitsubishi diesel engines below. A cloud of black smoke trailed behind it and when the winds were confused, the smoke wrapped around the ship.

The cargo from Saigon were mostly foods: vats of *nước mắm*, quartered pigs, and crates of mangoes. The imports back to Vietnam were more refined: Women's lacy underwear and Hong Kong cosmetics, which fetched ample profits for the middlemen.

I slept on a bunk bed amid the engine noise and cigarette smoke, but my dreams were fantastic. I dreamt of a world beyond the streets of Saigon, their distant thunder of bombs and random bursts of gunfire. I dreamt of going from port to port, to exotic lands, to hear countless foreign languages.

I was in awe of the ocean's salty and liquid vastness. Its solitude was new to me. Everywhere around, I saw water, velvety black, deep, and alive with waves, large and small. At night, flying fish skipped ahead of the bow like swallows, darting arrows in slivers of moonlight. Above us, the expanse of sky lit the world with stars, millions that I haven't seen since. I saw no land for hours on end. Uncle Đúng showed me charts, the compass and all the maritime instruments to locate the ship's position in the Pacific. "Here we are." He traced his finger along the S-shape curve of Vietnam's seacoast and then punched his finger down somewhere east of Nha Trang.

Then came the wonderful meals. Mr. Chen cooked the red snapper caught fresh that day, deep fried and coated in a sweet and sour sauce topped with thin slices of scallions and ginger. Other times, he stuffed squid with minced pork, diced onions and shitake mushrooms. Dinner was served in the captain's cabin and I was allowed to eat with the officers under the yellow lamps as the boat danced with the ocean's swells. It took me two days to get used to the changes in gravity as my stomach tried to hold the food down. Nobody else seemed to even notice the rocking. They walked in a cha-cha rhythm, one big step forward and then a couple of quick steps in between. *Give me time,* I told myself this is the life I wanted when I grew up: to be a merchant marine like Uncle Đúng.

My aunt, Ma's older sister, complained bitterly about his long absences at sea. "He left me with the kids to feed and wash. They will become vagabonds without their father. Why can't he find a job on land like most men?" Half of her prophecies came true, and she never forgave him for his profession. My three boy cousins were the opposite of my brothers and me. They skipped school, did drugs, and joined gangs. I used to envy them for the sense of irresponsibility that I was never allowed to have. Ma had trained us in the disciplined life of monks. To this day, I can't stop guilt pangs every time I buy something expensive or treat myself to a fine restaurant. My aunt was either too liberal or a real softie: she let her kids get away with everything and blamed Uncle Đúng instead. Even though they stayed in the same house together for the rest of their lives, my aunt and uncle never spoke much unless they had to sign some documents together.

The year after the trip down the coast of Vietnam, I embarked on a journey into the unknown. All my young life, I had been sheltered under Ma's watchful eyes, and suddenly, the gates swung open, and I found myself liberated, with total freedom I didn't even know existed. With fifty kids fresh out of high school, I went to Australia for college with all expenses paid. Suddenly, I could do just about whatever I wanted. I grew my hair long, bought hippie bell-bottom jeans, smoked a few cigarettes, and drank beer. Nobody was watching over my shoulder.

The Colombo Plan scholarship program gave us a short list of skills they believed Vietnam might need for restoration when the war was over. Most of my cohorts went for mechanical and chemical engineering, food science, and computer programming. I looked for anything that had to do with the ocean, but none was offered. I kept looking at the list and fixed my eyes on Forestry. I checked the box. None of my cohorts chose it, as I later found out. I had no idea back then what I wanted to do. The idea of being out in the woods, among wildlife, camping under the open sky was right for me. When I wrote to tell my father my choice, he thought I was foolish. "You should pick engineering for well-paying jobs. Who needs a forester in Vietnam? They are cutting down all the forests and selling off timber right now. There is nothing to manage." I didn't care. It was the first decision I made on my own.

It turned out that it was a decision I made casually, but one that shaped my entire life. Later, when I came to the U.S., I continued my education at UC Berkeley in environmental sciences and ended up working as a scientist for the U.S. Forest Service for thirty years. I spent most of my time in a lab and office analyzing data and publishing in scientific journals. It wasn't the outdoor lifestyle I fantasized about when I began forestry training. However, I took many trips to the field to study fire in the West, oak regeneration in the East, and insect and disease problems everywhere. I have seen all corners of the country, and let me tell you a secret; I packed a fly rod with me wherever there was a rumor of fish. Having access to Forest Service land and local fish biologists helped fuel my passion for the outdoors.

A long time passed when Uncle Đúng and I didn't see each other, but through two very different paths, we both ended up migrating to California. I found him and his family again in San Jose, where they settled after escaping the *Giải Phóng* of South Vietnam and spending a year locked up in a refugee camp in Hong Kong. While my aunt worked for a wealthy friend who owned a jewelry store in downtown San Jose, Uncle Đúng struggled to find what to do with his time.

For a while, he pumped gas and did handyman work for the apartment complex to help pay the rent until one day a friend offered him a gig as a mechanic on a ship exploring for oil in the Pacific and the North Sea. Once again, he was back at sea for months on end. This time, my aunt didn't mind because all the kids had grown up and got into trouble on their own. Their sons were society's problem now. She no longer had to worry that they would be killed in the jungle someplace.

Then Uncle Đúng got old and lost his eyesight to glaucoma. He lay in bed all day at a nursing home in the Vietnamese neighborhood behind Little Saigon in San Jose. I visited him several times when he still remembered my name. Although he couldn't see me, his hearing was intact. He was so glad to have a visitor, so rare for most elderly people in nursing homes. He held my hand tight. "Con Xê," he used my nickname—that's what I was called as a boy back home. My parents nicknamed us alphabetically, Xê is the French sound for C, and I am number three. "Do you live here now? How is your wife? Are you still working for the same office?" His mind was lucid. I fed him a bottle of yogurt, and he savored every spoonful.

"Uncle Đúng, do you remember the *Trường Hải*? You took me with you one time from Saigon to Da Nang?" He smiled. I asked him to tell me stories about his farm because he could talk endlessly about it.

"My family farm in the Mekong, we grew pineapples, the sweetest kind. We had jackfruits, longans, coconuts, and bananas too. But the pineapples were the best. They were small, the size of my fists, but they packed a punch. The juice would knock you over. My mother used to stir fry squid in tomato sauce and Chinese celery with a few slices of pineapple for sweetness." Then he felt for my arm and gripped the wrist "Con Xê, will you take me home?"

"I want to go home." He would not let go of my arm. I was sure he didn't mean the house in San Jose, and I would take him back to his farm if I could.

My aunt had already died the year before, and no one had the heart to tell him. His youngest daughter, Be Ha, came to the nursing home every day to bring him some home-cooked food to remind him of a taste of *nước mắm*. His sons never came even once.

He went home, finally. Not to the farm in Vietnam but to a green hill in San Jose. Be Ha made all the arrangements and put an obituary in the local Vietnamese newspaper. To our surprise, hundreds attended his funeral. A long line of people in black, old men and women, their children around my age, and they came with their children and grandchildren. They came to pay their respects.

"Your uncle saved our lives," one elderly man said, bowing to us with his hands together like a steeple. "Hundreds of us. We were at the docks fighting for a way to get out. All navy boats had already left with their families. The Viet Congs had taken over the city, we were the last to leave."

They talked about him and the last days of Saigon. He loaded the *Trường Hải* with refugees and took them to Hong Kong. That was the last trip he made with the boat and his crew. After surrendering the ship to Hong Kong police, the refugees were transported to a camp where they spent months and years with thousands of others, waiting for sponsors to get them out.

I haven't fulfilled my dream of becoming like uncle Đúng. Instead of the ocean, I have been to many mountains and meadows. Instead of watching flying fish darting ahead of the bow, I stalk rainbow trout in canyon streams. I still look at stars in the falling light over the Ponderosa pines and think of my own life adventures, and they all started with that trip down the sea coast of Vietnam.

Be Ha rested her head on my shoulder. I wrapped my arm around her to offer comfort. "I am relieved for Dad. His suffering was atrocious, not just his body but his mind. He was always alone. He was alone at sea and was alone at home. He never said much, but I know he loved us. He just didn't know how to show it."

"I know," I squeezed her shoulder a bit tighter. "He is with the ocean now," she said. "He is free to sail wherever he wants to go. He is on his way home."

Floating Lanterns

"Hue, Saigon, Hanoi, one country and yet so distant," the popular Vietnamese song goes. I was born near Hue, grew up in Saigon, and had only heard about Hanoi. The war had been over for a couple of decades when I finally visited Hanoi for the first time. The city was famous for its old quarter, with streets named after the wares that had been sold there for generations. Every house had a storefront, and people lived in apartments above them. One street displayed long bamboo poles, wooden posts, and planks. Another sold aluminum pots and pans. I stayed at a small hotel on *Hàng Gà* or Chicken Street, and the stores on that street still sold live chickens everywhere. Almost every corner was a wet market, open early in the morning and later in the afternoon. Shading these narrow streets, the *Bàng* tropical almond leaves the size of dinner plates were turning brown in the cooling autumn.

Maria and I sat on a bench looking at the Turtle temple and its reflection in the glassy Hoan Kiem Lake. It's an iconic view of the city in hundreds of photographs and postcards. We landed in Hanoi the day before, and this was the first day of rest so we could get acclimated. Everywhere we went, she stood out as the tallest woman in the whole city of Hanoi. Free of any makeup, she was tanned and athletic, probably a runner. I met her in Washington, DC, at a convention for Chicano writers. My friend Elvia in the Forest Service dragged me to it. "I want you to meet my friend. She is writing about Vietnam." So, I met Maria and we plotted this trip together.

"I am trying to finish my book," Maria said, her voice thick as the fog over the lake. "One more chapter to write, but I can't finish it."

"This trip will give you ideas," I hoped. That was one reason I wanted to be her guide and companion.

"Do you know that more Hispanic kids died in Vietnam than their fair share?" she asked. "Also Black kids. They got drafted, but many volunteered. Poor people, uneducated people, new immigrants, people without privilege," she continued. "Tony died here, and I want to retrace his steps."

I knew she mentioned her brother in her earlier book *La Frontera* about her home in Nogales, a city with the Mexican/American border running right through it.

Maria and I had talked about living in la Frontera, both literally and in the mind. I, too, straddle the border between the world I left behind and my current life as a Việt Kiều. The mind is a sticky trap: it refuses to let go of the past, no matter how hard we try to be in the present.

The old quarter in Hanoi with its storefronts and shade trees reminded me of the literature I had read while growing up in the South. I told Maria a classic story written by Nhat Linh, a novelist and a subversive revolutionary who deplored the poverty under French colonialism. I will never forget the story about two orphan boys huddling in the cold, collecting dried leaves to sell. Without money to buy coal, people burned *Bàng* leaves for heat. Every time a cold wind blew, the boys ran out after the fallen leaves and stuffed them in their sacks. Wet and shivering, they prayed: "Oh God, please, please send us more gusts."

A few kids ran around where we sat, and one came over to sell me the Canon lens cap I had just lost. I gave him a dollar, and he ran away, giggling. A few young girls struck up a conversation with Maria. "Can we speak English with you?" Maria smiled. She was a good teacher. These children were born after the war, so they had no bad feelings toward us.

On this first trip to Hanoi, I felt like a total stranger even though I could speak the language and understand all the street signs. Twenty years after the war ended, older people in the North still eyed foreigners with indifference and sometimes hostility. I can't blame them. Americans dropped bombs on them. The day before, when we were a bit lost, I asked an old lady for directions back to the hotel. "We don't live here either," she snapped sarcastically without looking at me. In the South, it was all about business, an open friendliness for deal-making. In Hanoi, foreigners were not always welcome.

I explained that attitude to Maria. Hanoi had been fighting wars for as long as the country existed. They had always worried about China to their north, and the border conflicts had gone on for at least a thousand years. Vietnamese kings had kowtowed to the Chinese emperor to ensure tenable peace or face an onslaught. They fought the French occupiers for one hundred years, then the Americans for another twenty years. Independence and reunification had been costly. I grew up in the South with abundant food from the Mekong Delta and supplies from the U.S. The North sacrificed all they had to the war with the single purpose of taking over the South. "At all costs," they pledged, and they finally succeeded in 1975.

Hanoi, Hue, and Saigon are often depicted in paintings as three women dressed in different costumes. The Hanoi woman is dressed in flowing silk garments and a round headdress the size of a lotus leaf. The Hue woman dons a white *Áo Dài,* an answer to the Chinese cheongsam but less colorful and sexier because the side slit comes up above the waist to reveal a delta of skin above the silk pantaloons. The Saigon woman is a peasant in a plain white tunic and black bottom, practical for working in the field. If I were to redesign the image to fit their current personalities, Hanoi would be a widow dressed in black.

We spent a couple of days visiting old temples and pagodas around Hanoi. Much had been destroyed or long neglected and now was being restored to a gaudy newness with red and gold paint. The wooden Thê Húc bridge was newly repainted and looked odd against the grimy buildings around Hoan Kiem Lake. We stopped at the Temple of Literature, where famous scholars were buried. The statues of the two warrior gods guarded the gate to every pagoda and protected the Buddhist followers. One smiled gently, and the other stared at us with fire coming out of his eyes. Inside, people burned incense and gold paper money in a cloud of acrid smoke. Maria bought a bundle of joss sticks and lit a few. She dropped money in the alms box and watched people offer food and incense to the gods and pray for the lost souls. Since that visit, she wanted to stop at every pagoda whenever possible to pay her respects.

"I must go see the DMZ soon. When can we leave?" The Demilitarized Zone was the dreaded place where intense fighting occurred when I was growing up in the South. It was also where Maria said Tony was stationed.

"I am renting a car and a driver. We leave tomorrow morning, three AM sharp," I said.

That morning I hired a man named Kien to drive us for one week. He came highly recommended by the hotel manager, who seemed very well connected to everyone around town, including the government. Kien was a skinny man about my age of forty, who owned an old Toyota and ran his own business. "Have car, will travel."

"Don't worry. I know every town in this country. I have driven every road from North to South. Many times," he waved an unlit cigarette. He had the sinewy and lanky toughness of a mountain lion. I bet he had been in the military and was sure he had killed.

"I can pay you fifty dollars a day. We need you for the week to make the trip to the DMZ and back," I said. He nodded agreement. It was a good deal considering most people were making a dollar a day selling a few vegetables in the farmers' market. He offered me a cigarette but I declined. I introduced him to Maria and he didn't shake her hand. I told him that if he needed to tell her anything I would be happy to translate for him. He shrugged.

We left the hotel in the dark. In the headlights, we saw people hauling their fruits, vegetables, live chickens, and chunks of pork on their bicycles. Street vendors carried baskets on their shoulders, bouncing along the sidewalks. They were coming in as we headed out of Hanoi and southward along Highway 1, which runs along the spine of the S-shaped country. This was the journey that I had dreamt about for so many years, as in an anti-war song by Trịnh Công Sơn:

When peace comes,
I will walk from Saigon to the central highlands,
from Hanoi to the South.

Vietnam had already been divided before I was born, and the only world I knew was south of the 17th parallel. This trip would fulfill my desire to see the other half of the country I had not been allowed to visit before.

Kien slipped a cassette into the dashboard player. "This is new Hanoi music. Have you heard this song before?" he asked me in his northern accent. I had been enjoying the way people talked in the North, with a sing-song cadence that's both alluring and biting. It can be sweet but may also cut like a scalpel depending on how they feel about you. The singing was even better than the way they talked. The lady's voice was a mix of operatic training and the soft growl of a cat, smoky as a blown-out candle. It was the way Hanoi women talk that can make your heart race, and want to marry them. Saigon people are loud and straightforward. It is like comparing Mandarin to Cantonese: one is finesse, the other all business.

Kien managed the traffic with one hand on the steering wheel and the other on the horn to blast away any obstacle. In America, he could be a great NASCAR driver. There was not a single car, truck, motorcycle, or buffalo that he didn't pass. Every ten miles, or so it seemed, we crossed a checkpoint. The guards carrying AK-47s waved us down, and Kien produced a document that quickly passed the inspection. They lifted the gate, and he sped away without a hassle. I wondered what Kien did before to earn such privilege. I was glad I got myself a tough and experienced employee.

The first night we stopped to check into a mini hotel on the side of Highway 1. It was a three-story house with rooms for rent. I offered Kien a room all by himself. He declined. "I will sleep in the hammock and watch the car. Do you want to go get a massage?" he asked.

"Here? In this small village. Do they have massage parlors?" My body was aching all over from a long day of sitting in the car over bad roads, but my Catholic background prevented me from saying yes. Having a woman touch me just seemed sinful.

He looked at me with a quizzical eye and lowered his voice, "You should sample the local flavors, North, Central, South. They are different."

I now got what he meant. "Nah, you go do what you want. I am going to have dinner with my friend and then go to bed." With that, he took off, and from then on, he just disappeared every night.

Maria and I found a roadside restaurant in town and ordered chicken noodle soup. That's all they had on the menu. An old steam-engine train hooted and came down the track along the other side of the highway. It came from the north, trailing a large white cloud behind. Somehow, like the people, it survived all the wars and kept on rolling. The noodle soup was thin, with a few slices of chicken with sharp bones and yellow skin. Unlike Perdue chicken with big soft breasts, the chicken in Vietnam feed on insects, worms, and a few grains of rice, and they are really skinny and tough. I always avoid the fatty chicken skin in America, but here, it was the best part of the whole meal.

"I don't think Kien likes me," Maria put her chopsticks down.

"He doesn't speak English," I replied, still looking for the last bit of skin in my bowl.

"No, he doesn't even look at me. He avoids me. He doesn't want to be seen with me."

"Do you want me to ask him?" I swallowed the last bit of the soup.

"No need. Maybe I remind him of the enemy. I don't blame him, though. I am the tall alien woman here."

"Me too. People here know exactly who I am by the way I talk and the way I look. I am a Việt Kiều, a Vietnamese with a U.S. passport. In some places, I am second-class. They fear you. They despise me."

"Really? I thought you should be higher than me."

"Just look at the way they treated you at the airport. They let you through quickly and me, they asked many questions. They always give you a nicer hotel room than me. You see?"

She nodded.

We got up early the next day and continued cruising south on Highway 1. The sun rose like a red ball over the Pacific and cast a glow on the tall mountain peaks. They stand as natural borders between Vietnam and China to the north and Laos to the west. We were in the thin stretch of land my high school history teacher called the long neck of the "skinny woman in the straw hat." Between the mountain range and the ocean, these northern provinces were miles of sandy beaches and narrow strips of farmland, barely enough to grow food. We passed fishing villages where the air smelled strongly of salt and fermented fish. Unlike the Mekong Delta in the South, the North has a much smaller Red River Delta to barely grow enough rice to feed their people. The Northerners had to make their living by fishing, coal mining, and cutting trees. That made them tough.

Kien slipped the same cassette tape into the dashboard. The lovely voice continued to lure me into a dream as it did the whole trip. This music was new and much happier than I grew up with. It was about love but not lost love, home but not morbid, and country but not war. Later, I kicked myself for not buying the tape from Kien, but I didn't even think of it at the time. I was so hypnotized by the limestone mountains on one side and the ocean on the other. We passed village after village, and I could tell what they grew by the crops they sold in stalls along the roadside.

We arrived at the village of Vinh Moc after another day of driving. Just north of the DMZ, it is famed for the network of deep tunnels that villagers dug to hide from the bombings. A petite woman guided us through the claustrophobic hole in the ground, barely wide enough for a person walking with head bent. In some places, the tunnel widened to about three feet.

"This used to be the space for a family gathering," she explained. "There lived sixty families down here at one time, and seventeen children were born during those years. The bombs could penetrate ten meters of earth, so they dug down to thirty meters."

We stayed overnight in Vinh Moc, and Kien disappeared right after we checked in. He didn't come to see us at our usual time the morning after. I waited with Maria in a small roadside hut having coffee and a bowl of Phở. Finally, Kien showed up, his eyes bloodshot.

"What's up? Did you find a massage parlor?"

"I am so sorry. I met some buddies last night. This is my village. I drank with them, and then we talked and talked about things, just catching up."

"You grew up here?" I asked.

"I fought in the war. My family died here. The American bombs took out everything above ground. Everything and everyone. Last night, I went to visit their graves and burned incense for them. I got drunk. I had to."

I offered him a hot coffee, a small baguette, and fried eggs. I let him take his time to eat and smoke a cigarette before we resumed our journey.

We crossed the Hien Luong bridge that spanned over the Ben Hai River. Officially, that used to be the boundary between North and South. Other than a monument to signify the landmark, the bridge was not unlike the other short bridges over small rivers that I had crossed in Vietnam. *That's it?* I thought. *Why did so many die here? Why did Vietnam get divided in the first place? The country north of this bridge is no different from its southern neighbor. Why two countries? Why did we fight each other to stay separate? Who did this to us?*

Maria grabbed my hand as we made this transition from North to South. We were right in the DMZ. The fighting was the fiercest south of here. U.S. troops fought for every hill and every town south of here. We stopped to look at the bombed-out church that remained gutted like the Atomic Dome in Hiroshima. Maria took pictures of the kids selling trinkets, and fake Zippos engraved with words like: "We are the fucking marines" and "If you are not with the one you love, love the one you're with."

Khe Sanh was our destination in the DMZ. A few miles from the border with Laos, this military base was the scene of a bloody siege with twenty thousand U.S. troops surrounded by three times as many Vietnamese hidden in the hills. Kien let us off at what used to be the airstrip. After twenty years of peace, the only thing recognizable of the base was the runway of red earth where no grass had grown back. The carcasses of a Chinook and a Huey helicopter were overgrown with vines of morning glory. All the instruments had been removed and the metal skeletons were held together with rust. There might be a few snakes inside their bellies.

It was all peaceful now. We stood there listening to the screeching of the macaques in the surrounding forests. Once, the Vietnamese were firing their cannons from these hills and the U.S.

carpet bombed them from B-52s. The battle of Khe Sanh was supposed to be the decisive one like Dien Bien Phu in 1954 that forced the French to surrender. Today, historians are saying that Khe Sanh was only a ruse, a costly distraction to keep the U.S. busy while the North Vietnamese staged all-out attacks on major cities in the Tết Offensive in 1968. I thought of Kien along with his buddies huddling on the hillside, firing rockets down on the base between U.S. bombing raids.

Maria pulled out the rest of the incense sticks that she had not yet burned along the way. She lit them and gave us a few each. She knelt down and planted them in the red dirt one by one in the shape of a smoking heart.

"This is where Tony died," she said. "My kid brother was only eighteen. They brought him home to Texas but I couldn't see him. His remains were in a closed coffin, draped with the American flag." She wiped her eyes. For the first time, Kien reached out and held her hand. We formed a circle in silence amid the incense smoke and the heat rising from the red earth.

Before returning home, we spent a day playing tourists in Hue. We paid our respects to many more pagodas and burned incense in every temple. We saw the restoration work underway at the Citadel that was destroyed during Tết of 1968. That night in Hue, Kien did not disappear to find his favorite massage parlors. He took us to a restaurant run by people who are deaf and mute from birth. They cooked and served in an eerie silence. Kien ordered for us authentic rice cakes cooked in banana leaves and stuffed with minced onion and ground pork. Only Hue people can make the cakes so thin you can see the insides through the translucent rice dough. The fish sauce dip was pungent, mixed with chopped garlic, red hot chili pepper, sugar, and a dash of lemon juice, just the way my mother made it. Then we caught the last act for the night aboard a wooden boat on the Perfume River. A cottage industry of tourism had started in Hue with a small fleet of boats with musicians on board.

"This is authentic Hue music," Kien held Maria's hand to help her step down from the dock.

Against the backdrop of the Marble Mountain in the far distance, the river turned purple in the twilight. After some tea and a round of introductions, a pretty woman in a white Áo Dài played a one-string instrument made of a coconut shell mounted on a wooden sound box. She plucked the string with a bamboo pick while her other hand vibrated a lever to bend the haunting sound. Another lady brushed a sixteen-string bamboo koto with her long fingernails sending out cascades of rain on a tin roof. They sang in the heavy Hue accent. The songs painted pictures of school girls in white walking along the Perfume River with dreams in their heads and pressed flowers in their books while the flame trees bloomed red, and cicadas announced the arrival of summer.

After the performance, they lit small candles in paper boats and let us float them downriver.

"It is to guide the path for the dead," Kien explained. "Some need to find their way home."

I said a quiet prayer for Tony and Kien's family, the people of Hue, Saigon, and Hanoi who died fighting for both North and South, villagers who burned in the plasma of napalm, those who came from far-away countries and died here, and the boat people who didn't survive their escape to reach a refugee camp. The glowing lights formed little groups of stars, danced like fireflies, then they separated and wandered on, aimlessly, further and further away.

Dr. Ni

He is a man of the Mekong. Like the Delta itself, the people are known for being warm and honest. Straight as a horse's gut, as they say there. He speaks with a strong voice and simple words in short sentences, ending with "huh?" like the punctuation of a thought, a statement, or a question to make sure you understand before he goes on with the story. Everything is a story. It is the way he talks. It is the way he teaches.

"Do you know that I used to race turtles as a kid, huh?" He turned from the front passenger seat to face us in the back of the van. A few friends from the U.S. were with me for a tour of the Mekong Delta, and Dr. Ni was showing us around.

We always expected a joke from him because we don't always know whether he is serious or joking. He always speaks in the same tone.

"How do you race turtles? Must be a big event in Can Tho, I am sure," I kept my tongue firmly planted in my cheek, thinking of something as exciting as sumo wrestling or the Olympic curling competition.

"Yes, the biggest event here in town, especially when I used to organize it," he replied, deadpan.

We realized there was something to this story after all. It was funny but not a joke. So we all waited for him to continue. He looked straight ahead at the new highway dividing the country-side into two separate worlds that used to be one. I couldn't take the silence anymore and tapped on his shoulder to get him back to the topic at hand. He smiled and cleared his throat.

"First, you turn them upside down and lay them on the hot pavement, huh? Let them bake a little bit, then you turn them over." He looked at us to make sure we got it. We stared back at him. He smiled and continued.

"When they are thirsty, they run to the nearest body of water. So, you always race them near the river. They can tell where the water is. It is always downhill."

Brilliant! I had known this man to possess a body of local knowledge of the Mekong Delta. When I grew up in Saigon, I had not seen much of the South and simply knew the Delta as the rice basket that could feed the whole country. My only exposure was one summer in Can Tho, a quiet town on the south fork of the mighty Mekong River. My father was stationed there for a few years and I was happy to be with him for three months between school years. I spent many afternoons fishing the big river with a long bamboo pole and earthworms for bait. Who knows, Dr. Ni and I could have been two kids fishing from the same river bank.

I met Dr. Ni on my first trip back to Vietnam in 1994. I came to the Mekong as a volunteer for the International Crane Foun-dation to help restore Tram Chim National Park, the wintering ground for the Eastern Sarus Crane. Around the 7000-hectare protected area of the Park, villagers lived in rickety bamboo huts in the buffer zone. That's where Dr. Ni operated. Trained as an ecologist and a social scientist, Dr. Ni spent his time helping local people start small businesses. He ran a micro-financing program with modest funding from UK collaborators, and his program was a rare success. Most environmental and humanitarian projects did not survive the endemic corruption in Vietnam.

"Welcome home, Anh Hao," he shook my hand and smiled. I felt the sincerity radiating from his face. "Here is where the action is. If the people can make a living, huh? They will protect the cranes."

Before I came to Tram Chim, I had only a textbook knowledge of sustainability as a three-legged stool—a balance of ecological, economic, and social elements. Here, Dr. Ni showed me how that worked.

"You know, one hundred dollars is not much in the U.S., but it can make a big difference here, huh? But you have to do it the right way; otherwise, once the money is given out, it is gone."

"So, tell me how you do it?" I asked.

"First, I never give the money to the men. They will drink and gamble it all. I only work with the women committees. They make sure the money is used to help the family and their kids. They always repay us, so we can use the money again many times."

Vietnamese men are famous for their irresponsibility. They smoked, drank, and womanized. Society allowed these bad habits because of their gender, but not in my household. My mother did not tolerate any abuse by my father or any man and would talk back. He usually backed off and retreated to his corner, fixing watches and radios. She was perhaps one of the first feminists in Vietnam. She had driven a car across the Hai Van pass between Danang and Hue when her father was alive and wealthy. His Cantonese merchant culture gave her the fearlessness rare in women of her time. However, except for a few who were deemed henpecked, most men were entitled to rule households like kings. If they didn't get what they wanted, they could go seek that somewhere else. My mother made sure I did not become like that.

"Second, I tell them it is their money. They will not waste it because it is theirs, not mine."

"Third, I always give out money in broad daylight. We have a public meeting and record the ceremonies when I transfer funds. That way, everyone knows that there is no hidden agenda, I did not pocket any of it, and they are accountable to the community to make the money work."

Later, I walked around the village with Dr. Ni and he pointed out the barbershop, the pig farm, and the workshop where women wove the exquisitely shaped conical hats with sixteen concentric rings and a hidden poem pressed between the dry palm leaves.

I always wonder why Dr. Ni is different from so many corrupt government officials in Vietnam. Corruption is systemic and engrained in our DNA. Emperors and kings amassed wealth through a system of mandarins and officials and kept the people poor and illiterate. Everyone was pocketing something for themselves whenever they could. Anyone who had control of your time, your money, or your life could demand a bribe. Forest rangers turned their backs on illegal logging in the rainforests. Generals took millions and created a ghost army of only names, no conscripts. Those who refused to join the corruption system lost their jobs or were never promoted. So it had been for thousands of years.

"What makes you choose to work in this poor province? With your degrees, you can make a lot more money in Ho Chi Minh City," I looked at his dusty white shirt, the only shirt color that I had ever seen him wear.

"I love it here. This is where I belong. Besides, what you do for these poor villages will last a long time." He swept his hand across the green landscape of rice fields and villages sheltered by tall bamboo hedges.

Before I left Tram Chim to go back home to the U.S., Dr. Ni pulled me aside and told me he wanted to show me something. I followed him down a dirt path for half a mile outside the village until we reached a lotus field. The flooded field stretched as far as the eye could see. Red flowers the size of dinner plates bloomed above a floating green mat of circular leaves. Dragonflies hovered in the gentle and fragrant breeze. He pulled a small, waterlogged wooden boat from the tall weeds and held it steady for me to get in. With a long bamboo pole, he pushed the boat out about a hundred yards and then it was just the two of us in the middle of the field. We rested for a while watching the dragonflies and enjoying the sweet scent of the flowers. The world seemed to stop turning and time stood still. We didn't say a word, but I understood what he wanted to tell me.

Later we said goodbye. "I am sure you will remember this place, huh?" He shook my hand with both of his.

Twenty years had passed since we first met. I saw him now and then at Tram Chim and witnessed the improvements he had made to the villages around the park. At one time, I brought him to the U.S. on a study tour to talk to my colleagues in the Forest Service about research ideas. It must have been fifteen years since I last saw him in America, although we occasionally exchanged emails. On this particular trip, my friends and I arrived in Can Tho to pick him up. We were fortunate that he could spend the week with us since he is the resident expert about the Mekong Delta.

Dr. Ni came out as our van pulled up to his farmhouse on the outskirts of the city. He had not changed at all and neither had I, despite a bit more hair loss. We embraced like two little school kids who had been away from each other the whole summer. "Please stay one night here in Can Tho and we can leave tomorrow morning. I have reserved a place for dinner tonight on the river."

My friends and I checked into a downtown hotel and met up with Dr. Ni and his wife later that evening. "Welcome back, Anh Hao." She remembered me from my previous trip. She hadn't changed much, still the same gentle smile on a sunburned face free of makeup. She wore a white blouse matching his shirt. Then they walked with us toward the riverbank. I had always loved Can Tho, a gentle city on the south fork of the Mekong River. It had grown a lot since the time I was a kid, but it still had quiet corners that reminded me of the way life used to be. The restaurant was one of those.

Under the banyan trees, we had our dinner in a private gazebo. Dr. Ni ordered local specialties, starting with a fried tofu that melted in the mouth, mimosa flowers stir-fried with shallots, baked eggplants dipped in fish sauce, and a hot pot with fresh caught fish in a boiling broth of star fruit and tamarind.

"Now, let me give you a special treat: this is the heart and soul of the Mekong," Dr. Ni said. He told the wait staff that we were ready for the entertainment. They went away and came back with a couple of musicians.

"These are two local artists. Meet Anh Tuan and his wife Lan," Dr. Ni said. We bowed to them and they bowed back.

"My wife and I are Vọng Cổ musicians. I hope you like Vọng Cổ," Anh Tuan said.

Anh Tuan was a thin man, my age, with gray hair and a thin beard. It is unusual for a Vietnamese to have a full beard but he came close. A good-looking man despite his rough clothing and sunburnt complexion. He offered me a cigarette but I declined. Everybody smokes in Vietnam and every conversation or business begins with an exchange of cigarettes.

"You must be Anh Hao. How do you like Vietnam?" He knew I was a Việt Kiều.

"I love Vietnam. I come back often to see my friends and family," I said.

I was more interested in the Vọng Cổ music than talking. Vọng Cổ was very popular when I was a kid growing up here fifty years ago. Radio stations played Vọng Cổ every Saturday night and I used to lie in bed with a transistor radio pressed to my ear. It came back to me when I returned to Vietnam for the first time after twenty years. One night in Tram Chim National Park, I sat on a canal levee with a park ranger watching the egrets glide home in the twilight. Across the water in a guard house someone was cooking dinner and the smell of burned fish sauce was wafting in my direction along with the sound of Vọng Cổ music. The glowing kerosene lamp lit a corner of the world and the warm air embraced me. The music with simple words of the peasants and their feelings in honest, fresh, and heartrending lyrics accompanied by the nuanced sounds of the Vietnamese guitar welcomed me home.

"Now let us hear Anh Tuan play," Dr. Ni got the show going.

Anh Tuan pulled from the black bag the old guitar and tuned it by ear. It was an acoustic guitar with five steel strings that looked like a Martin from a distance, but the most peculiar part about the guitar was its fretboard. The wood was carved deep and hollow between the fret wires to allow the player to bend the sound by pressing down deeper on the strings.

With a pick he plucked the metal strings in fast successions. Sometimes it sounded like firecrackers at Tết, at times a mellow cadence, sometimes deep thumping like drum beats. In between long runs, he punctuated the lines with the wooden foot castanet. Anh Tuan and Lan sang a few duets written for both voices. They traded back and forth a flirty conversation between two peasants in playful courtship.

"I have one special request. Can you play the 'Lament of the Straw Mat Vendor?'" I asked. It was one that I remembered well from childhood.

"Yes, that's a classic. One of the most beloved songs of the Mekong. One may say it is the soul of the South," Dr. Ni said.

Anh Tuan sang the lament, his voice deep and sorrowful. The piece was written for a male voice about a boatman who traveled up and down the Mekong River selling straw mats. One day he met a beautiful girl who asked him to come to her house. She showed him her bedroom and asked him to make her a pair of special mats. He spent many months weaving the most beautiful mats to please her, but when he came to deliver the mats, she had already left the village to marry someone faraway. He put the mats back in his wooden boat and vowed never to sell them.

The next morning, we headed west to Tram Chim National Park. As we drove up to the guesthouse to unload our luggage, Mr. Hùng came to greet me and shook my hands with both of his. "Hello, Anh Hao, remember me?" Of course, I did. He and I were sitting on a levee counting birds together one evening twenty years ago. He was now director of the park and managed all the staff of a hundred employees.

"Tomorrow, we will get up early. I will show you around. The cranes have not returned yet, but there are many other birds to see," Hùng said.

Six o'clock the next morning, just as the sun was about to rise, Dr. Ni and I boarded a long wooden boat and toured the park with Mr. Hùng. White clouds of pond herons took off ahead of our boat. The number of wetland birds had increased so much thanks to the protection by Mr. Hùng and his staff. The blue hens were nesting in the reeds. Kingfishers flashed their neon blue wings over the canal in search of minnows. Outside the park borders, the bamboo huts I saw years ago had been replaced by brick and cinder block buildings. The rickety toilets hanging over the canals were long gone. All the dirt roads had been paved now. Back then, the government guest house was the only two-story concrete block structure towering over the low-lying and flat landscape. From the top of that house now, we no longer had a 360-degree view of the fields and direct sight of the cranes in the distance.

So, one might say progress had been made.

"This place has changed so much, Anh Ni. What happened?"

"What you see is the development everywhere in Southeast Asia and it is not necessarily good," Dr. Ni lamented.

Being an ecologist is depressing. We see everything as an issue. "Look at the way we grow rice today." He waved his arm across the endless industrial rice fields stretching to the horizon. Twenty years back, this landscape was all small farms and villages surrounded by bamboo hedges, cemeteries, fish ponds, and canals. No water buffalo rolled in the mud any more. No people waded in the muddy field planting rice with their bare hands. He pointed out roadside signs of chemical companies boasting three rice crops a year. Large processing plants every few miles employed hundreds of workers. Instead of owning their own farms and growing their own crops, they now worked in factories turning out perfectly packed fifty-pound bags.

"Do you know why we have to forgive the U.S. for the harmful effects of Agent Orange, Agent White, and all the defoliants used in the war, huh? Because the amount of chemicals being used today far exceeds that used in the war. Chemical companies have data. We don't. They win."

Better living through chemistry, I thought. U.S. Agricultural companies are leading the way. The USDA even calls it "conventional agriculture" with Roundup-ready crops and scientific applications of chemicals. And I always thought that organic farming was conventional.

"It is a false dichotomy," Dr. Ni drove the point home. "We trade productivity for a loss of diversity of species and culture. There used to be hundreds of varieties of rice, now there is one. There used to be family farms, now there is one company. We wiped out the insects and the birds too."

As we drove south toward the southern tip of the Delta, the land changed from a freshwater wetland to a coastal ecosystem. Rice fields disappeared as vast aerated ponds became the dominant features in the landscape.

"Look! This area used to be mangrove forests once. Now you see only shrimp farms. Sea water used to flow in and out naturally with the tides, now it is all stagnant. No more natural cleansing of the soil. The decayed food and waste accumulate and it takes only three years for the system to crash. Just like shifting cultivation in the highlands, people abandon their farms and move on to deforest more mangrove forests. The defoliated mangrove forests did come back after the war and now we lose them all to shrimp farming. What we lose now is lost forever," there was no humor in his voice.

"The issues are too big here. China is building dams upstream. They will alter the water flow and kill the migratory fish. Second problem, our dependence on chemicals is irreversible and God knows what health effects we will see. And third, sea level rise. Half a meter and this whole delta is under water."

My friends and I stayed quiet with the gravity of what we heard. We are educated tourists, and we thought we had answers to everything.

Every evening, we came to another small town and checked into a mini-hotel. For dinner, Dr. Ni made sure we had local foods cooked at some special place that he liked. "Do you like the fish we eat?" he switched to a more cheerful topic. "They are small but delicious. You know? We used to complain that poor people eat small fish and rich people in cities eat bigger fish. Now we know that wild and smaller fish pack more nutrients. Bigger fish are farm raised and tasteless. There is justice in all this, huh? That's the way of life here in the Mekong Delta. People used to catch fish in the rice fields and rivers. Soon, there will be no wild fish anymore, huh?"

Night fell and we reached the Cape of Ca Mau, the southern-most tip of Vietnam. When I grew up, all that I heard about this place was about how dangerous and desolate it was: where mosquitoes sing like flutes and leeches swim thick like rice noodles. That reputation was no longer true. Many people had come to settle here after the war and made it another bustling urban center.

We huddled around another authentic dinner with a hot pot of tuna fish cooked with banana flowers, boiled morning glory shoots dipped in fish sauce, fried tofu, and grilled eggplant.

"Do you know that our food and the way we eat is very participatory, huh?" Dr. Ni was in teaching mode again. We waited.

"Do you see, in the U.S. everyone eats from their own plates. Here, we share. We put into the hot pot what we want to eat, but we share the broth and there is a variety of what we can add to it. Huh?"

After dinner, my friends still enjoyed one more round of Tiger beer. Dr. Ni pulled me aside. "Let's go get a cup of tea."

We went across the road to a small roadside teahouse that was still open. We sat on low plastic stools against a wall with a pot of tea between us. The city had gone to sleep and only a few Karaoke places still blared out music, mixed with the Vọng Cổ from neighboring radios.

"I have to tell you something personal," he began.

"Are you okay?" I was afraid he might have cancer.

"Remember the time I came to the U.S.? You invited me to Washington, DC and then you drove me to your old research station in Wisconsin? Fifteen years ago, the year 2000. Huh?"

"Yes, I remember. It was a short trip. I had some funding from a grant and I wanted you to do some good with it."

"Do you know what I did with the money? Thousands of dollars? You never asked me for a report."

"I trust you, my friend. I don't need a report."

"Then I will tell you what I did after I came back from the U.S. Remember Hòa An, the village that you and I visited once. Huh?"

"Yes. You took me there to see the experimental Melaleuca forest area that you were managing. I remember drinking rice wine with the farmers, and I got so drunk I passed out in a hammock. I only had a few rounds and next thing I knew, I was out cold." I laughed and was relieved that Dr. Ni was not sick.

"They love you, Anh Hao. They remember you still, a Việt Kiều who shared with them a simple meal and their home brew. I will take you back there someday. Anyway, remember Hòa An?"

"Yes, I remember it was a small and poor village, very poor. They were distilling the essence from the Melaleuca leaves in big metal drums to sell as eucalyptus oil. The skinny Melaleuca timber was only good for fuel and not of much value. That was all the income they could make from the dwarf forest. The farmers were asking me questions about how to build a business, to get more from their land and I had no answers. I am educated in America, but that knowledge doesn't apply here." I held the tea cup with both hands.

"I asked them what they would need to do better. They said they needed education for their children. Without education, they would be poor forever. Now, they don't have that excuse."

He poured me more tea. I leaned forward for his next sentences and he took his time.

"With your money, I bought some land, dirt cheap. Then I found more funding and built a school. You should see it now. Hundreds of students. Fifteen of them have gone to college."

Tears welled up in my eyes and I had no words. I couldn't even sip from the cup of tea. Dr. Ni had honored me beyond measure. He had given Hòa An a precious gift: Hope. It was a priceless gift to me too. Somehow in that little roadside café near midnight, I could smell the red flowers and feel the light breeze among waving leaves in the lotus field near Tram Chim twenty years ago.

The Vọng Cổ music was in the air after the Karaoke had died down. I thought of Dr. Ni as a modern-day straw mat vendor. He loved the Mekong Delta the way the vendor loved that girl who did not love him back. She left for a life faraway in the same way the people had given up their traditional lifestyle in exchange for the promise of wealth. He wove the most beautiful straw mats of knowledge that nobody wanted. He holds them in his heart, and it is not for sale.

Ten Pounds of Pork

Many hues of green exploded before my lazy eyes. The wet rice fields glowed neon, coconut palms a dark, drab shade, and morning glory in fishponds a dusty brownish green. That's what I remember about the Vietnam countryside: green everywhere. Water buffaloes bathe in the canals that crisscross that landscape. In the distance from the window of the van, the conical outline of Bà Đen Mountain loomed like Mount Fuji but without the famous snow cap. A strange geological phenomenon, the basaltic mountain rises high up above the flat alluvial Mekong Delta.

We were heading west on the road to Tay Ninh nearest to the Cambodian border to visit my brother Hòa and his wife Phương. Tay Ninh is famous for the Cao Dai religion, with peculiar worship of the Buddha, Jesus Christ, Martin Luther King, Jr., and the Pope thrown in. The simple mention of Tay Ninh also brings memories of bloody battles between the U.S. and its allies against the Vietnamese guerillas as well as border conflicts between Vietnam and Cambodia. Finally, the Vietnamese government claimed the land for good by settling many ex-military families in the new-economic zone west of Tay Ninh where my mother and brothers came to live.

I often came back to pay respects to my mother, whose grave was among the first to be dug in a graveyard not far from Hòa's farm. I had traveled this road many times, and every time, I nervously watched out for speed traps and armed traffic cops waiting to hail us down for a bribe. Street vendors balancing heavy food baskets on bamboo sticks, chickens, dogs, and children crossed the road at any time. Every trip, I have seen a dead dog or chicken crushed by a truck, and, occasionally a bloody human body on the roadside rolled up inside a straw mat waiting to be identified.

The road from Saigon to Tay Ninh was known as the thoroughfare for *Buôn Lậu,* a term that describes all kinds of illegal commerce. On a previous trip to Tay Ninh, I asked Phương why people resorted to smuggling at all.

"We were all smugglers here. This is the border town where all things happened. We bought and sold anything we could to make money." Phương giggled as she told me stories about the earlier days when they first settled in Kinh Tế Mới, the new economic zone.

"Why did you have to smuggle?" I asked.

"There was nothing to buy in the market, not only because we produced nothing for years after the war but it was illegal to buy and sell. The government gave us a subsidy of barley and cassava at first and expected us to survive on that ration. Knowing that left alone, the people would create a free-market society, the government outlawed all commerce. We were told to produce rice even though the land was not ready for it. They didn't care if we starved. It was government policy that everyone must grow rice."

"Anh Hòa needed diesel and engine oil for the truck and the only way was to get it from across the border. He bought cigarettes rolled in Cambodia, fake Marlboros, and sold them here.

Some of them were loaded with opium. Anh Hòa and I worked at the brick factory across the street for a while, but we were just slaves for someone else. We made more money with the old truck working for ourselves and other farmers. On the side, we smuggled," she said in her sing-song voice.

"So, what else did people smuggle?" I wondered.

"Everything. Lots of opium, but mostly food because people were hungry. Meat, yes, pork. It took many years for us to cut down the trees and build up the soil, so we could get one crop of rice each year. We ate so much cassava our bellies swelled up like pregnant women. There was no meat, no rice. Not for many years. We ate barley mixed with sweet potato day in and day out," she almost cried. "Kinh Tế Mới was the end of the earth back then. We were prisoners here, nowhere else to go."

Before I boarded the van for the dreaded three-hour drive to Tay Ninh, I told the driver, "I don't care about when we get there. I don't want you to hit anyone, not even a chicken. I want you to drive within the speed limits. If you get stopped by the cops for speeding and they take your license, it is your problem. I will give you a good tip if you don't get us in trouble." He grinned, waving a cigarette.

And he really earned his tip. Not only did he drive carefully, he was a talkative know-it-all who entertained my companions and me with one story after another. My brother Hòa said drivers are great storytellers. Many of their stories are real; the rest they borrow from drinking friends they meet on their nights away from home. Regardless, captive for three hours in a small van, I had the time and it was worth it. He talked about the history of little towns we crossed, what's good to eat, where you find the best Phở, rice rolls, and restaurants serving wildlife dishes.

As we neared the town of Tay Ninh, I got more and more nervous, anticipating a few khaki-clad policemen with pistols on their hips waving batons to stop our van. They looked for the vans that had Việt Kiều us on board. However, there is nothing that a twenty-dollar bill can't fix. The drivers would slip them the money inside the paperwork to expedite the process.

"Look here, we are now arriving in Tay Ninh," the driver announced with a sweep of his hand.

He gently shifted down to about twenty miles an hour and confidently entered the town. Tay Ninh had improved every time I came back. The streets were wider, cleaner, and lined with trees. I saw a few policemen but they ignored us, no hassle at all.

"What's wrong?" I asked.

"Let me explain when we get to the next bend," the driver muttered. At the main roundabout in the middle of town, he pointed out to me a shrine mounted on the trunk of an old tamarind tree. Red sticks of incense and a few mangos adorned the altar.

"That is where Chị Sáu died two years ago," he began.

"Who is Chị Sáu?" I took his bait.

"She was the pork smuggler. Everyone here knows the story of the woman who changed this town forever. Since you were not here when this happened, let me give you the full account," he set the hook.

"The route we are on from Ho Chi Minh City to Tay Ninh and heading west to the Cambodian border has been famous for two things: traffic deaths and smuggling. The death count on this road is highest in the province and perhaps in the whole country because it is a major route for illegal imports from Cambodia. They used to smuggle lumber, cigarettes, food, and liquor. Now we have new commodities: cocaine, heroin, opium. Smuggling and traffic deaths go hand in hand." He sounded like a reporter for CNN.

"Smugglers are people just like us. They come from all walks of life, youths, ex-military, housewives, even kids. The tough ones drive trucks and souped-up motorbikes, and they often speed down this road in the dark of night. Smaller operators smuggle what they can carry on their bodies and travel in crowded buses. They even smuggle pieces of a pig, chicken, and dog even. Some hunt foxes and snakes to sell to specialty restaurants." He continued to spin his story.

"I was smuggling a bit myself. I survived the war. I was trained to drive trucks for the army and I had driven everywhere in Cambodia. I knew where poppies were grown and where they dried into the latex to make opium. I knew where fake Pall Malls and Salems were rolled. There was still easy money to be made in Saigon. Even back then, some people had plenty of money to feed their addictions. The corrupt cops in this town knew me since many of them were my comrades. When they saw my truck, I simply slowed down, showed them the papers with money stuck inside. Sometimes, I gave them a carton of cigarettes and they waved me on. It was not worth getting shot at," he boasted.

"The Tay Ninh police are the toughest law enforcement money can buy," he chuckled. "They set up speed traps and checkpoints along this road and stopped all traffic. In response, the gangs of smugglers used their own tactics of overwhelming force. They burst through town like kamikazes—a high speed human wave. The cops could not catch them all, but whenever they caught a truck or a motorbike loaded with contraband, brutality followed."

I believed him. In fact, I grew up fearful of our own soldiers, the Viet Cong, American troops, along with city police. I had seen corpses in the streets of Saigon during the Tết Offensive of 1968. I had been harassed by police for small bribes. I had seen kids blow their feet off with Carbine rifles. My friends got killed and came back from the jungles in body bags. Gun phobia is hard for me to shake. I don't care what is said about "serve and protect," the Vietnamese police have done more harm than good as far as I am concerned. I avoid them whenever possible. People with guns in remote towns like this are the worst.

The driver brought me back to his story. "The police would confiscate the goods, sell them in the black market to stuff their own pockets, and put the smugglers in jail until someone bailed them out. War was waged between smugglers and cops. Sometimes smugglers fired on the police. Nobody won. The death tolls rose on the road along with the corruption."

"The traffic is not so bad now. I don't see too many cops either. What happened?" I asked.

"Things have changed! Smuggling is still happening but the roadblocks and checkpoints are gone now. It is much better for drivers like me all thanks to one woman." He slowed down and opened his window for some fresh air.

"Two years ago, a young woman named Chị Sáu and a friend traveled along this route to buy and sell pork. She made her daily visit to a remote farm to buy a slab of pork belly to resell in her village. A few grams of meat would be a special treat for most people whose daily diet was boiled morning glory, cassava, and salted fish. She cut it up into thin strips and tied them to her legs and around her waist underneath her dark brown tunic. Her friend would keep her company and they pretended to be sisters going home to the farm to visit relatives.

"Country buses were the basic means of transportation for the poor. These antique Renaults had been repaired over and over again by self-taught mechanics. Parts were machined in local shops to replace worn-out gears. Rusted floorboards had been fortified with plywood. The rattling, creaks, exhaust, cigarette smoke, rotten fish, and excrement made these bus rides an experience only the desperate would tolerate. Sometimes, a loaded bus veered off the road killing about fifty people along with livestock and whoever happened to be hit.

"One day, their bus was stopped at a checkpoint and the cops unloaded everybody and everything. As usual, they confiscated cartons of cigarettes and drugs. Unfortunately for Chị Sáu, they did body searches and found the pork belly she was hiding. They booked her and threatened to throw her in the fetid jail along with all the other passengers.

"Chị Sáu pleaded, 'Please! This is all I have to feed my family. It is not much. You can keep the pork, and here is all the money I have, please take it, but let me go. I have two small children to feed. They need me home or they will starve. Please!' The two policemen kept holding her arms to keep her from getting away.

"Nothing she or her friend said made a difference to the men. The more they pleaded, the more interested the two policemen became in what they could do to the helpless women.

"The cops grinned, grabbed them by the waist, 'What's the hurry? Going home to the dirty peasant husbands of yours while you could have a good night's sleep here on a real bed? We know how to treat women right.'

"The midday sun bore down heavily on the asphalt and the tin roofs along the road. The overheated air loaded with vehicle exhausts, dust, and blaring horns would drive anybody insane. Dizzy and frightened by the harassment, Chị Sáu dashed out to the street like a wild deer.

"A convoy of military troops happened to drive by the town of Tay Ninh that day. They were returning to Ho Chi Minh City from a month of peacekeeping along the Cambodian border. A jeep followed by two trucks full of tired soldiers rumbled down the main street of town at a good speed, blasting their horns as they went.

"The lead jeep arrived at the checkpoint exactly when Chị Sáu ran across the road. She was hit straight on by the grill of the vehicle. Her head smashed, she died instantly.

"A colonel in a dusty uniform stepped down from the jeep to inspect the bloody scene. He saw the two cops, the crowd around the bus, and he had a sense of what happened. Colonel Minh was a famous soldier from the North who had fought long wars and was known throughout the country as one of the toughest and most respected among the troops. Now in his fifties, he had seen many battles and many deaths. He had a will of iron and a heart of a tiger. He had no family left to worry about and he wished for a better country that he was willing to die for, many times over. 'Who did this?' He barked.

"The friend grabbed his arm and told him Chị Sáu's story. She wiped her tears with her dirty sleeves, 'For a few kilos of pork to feed her family, she had to die. They killed her!' she pointed at the two cops.

"Colonel Minh looked at the young woman's mangled corpse lying between the front wheels. His frown deepened and his back stiffened. Without a word, he turned, drew his pistol and fired. The cops dropped to the ground. More blood soaked the dirty sidewalk. 'Go and round up all the filthy bastards in this town. Every one of them!' he ordered his troops.

"His men went looking for the rest of the town police, but by then word had spread and the cops had gone into hiding. The news of the military declaring war on the town police went national. The colonel turned himself into the Ho Chi Minh City police headquarters to await judgment for his actions.

"A court case was opened and after months of deliberation at the highest level, the colonel was judged to have acted fairly and was restored honorably to his rank. The two dead cops were ruled to have died in the line of duty, so that their families received death benefits.

"Since then, the town of Tay Ninh has a new sense of justice and is more welcoming to people who pass through." The driver said. "The police still watch out for speeders, drunkards, and drug smugglers. However, they really just stick to the business of traffic control. If you drive within the speed limits and watch the signs, they leave you alone."

A few town policemen in khaki uniforms eyed our van as we passed by the main street of Tay Ninh. They did not wave their batons or blow the whistles as we drove on. Our driver was silent for a few minutes as were all my companions in the van. Out the window, the different shades of green seemed to glow greener. The distant Bà Đen Mountain loomed severely over the landscape. A few more miles and we would reach my brother's mango farm, and my journey home would be complete.

We all were thankful to the woman who died there for a few pounds of pork. In silence we paid our respects.

The Boatman

"You should see the new tunnel. It only costs a few dollars for the extra five miles. You must see it while you are here," the taxi driver said. I had hailed his cab to get from my hotel in Saigon to visit a brother in the outskirts of the city.

I grunted approval. I wanted to see the modern marvel under the river connecting Saigon with the island of Thu Thiem. Everybody had been talking about the tunnel. It was built with World Bank money by Japanese engineers to the highest standards in the world.

The tunnel was well-lit, with two lanes each way, complete with blue and white signs to direct traffic to the right destinations. Two large stainless-steel propellers like aircraft turbines ventilated the underground structure. You would not believe that you were still in Vietnam, where most roads were full of potholes, and buffaloes and children crossed the heavy traffic to get to their village on the other side.

Coming out of the tunnel, we were in Thu Thiem, an island in the middle of the wide Saigon River that had been dredged deep enough for large cargo ships to dock. The new highway connecting the island with Saigon was lined on both sides with dwarf palms, the native vegetation. On the far side of the island, a few remaining huts made of cardboard, pieces of rusty metal, and coconut fronds littered the swampy landscape. It was only a matter of time before they would be removed to make room for more skyscrapers and condominiums.

"Look at those tall buildings!" The taxi driver pointed at the skyline.

"Americans and Việt Kiều are buying them up—half a million dollars for an apartment with a view of downtown Saigon," he continued. "The highway is so wide and smooth here the crazy kids come to race their motorcycles. There have been several deaths so they are no longer allowed to be on the island after dark."

I imagined the bloody game of motorcycle racing by youths high on drugs. They must feel no fear or pain. That's what it takes to race or fight.

"Do you live in America?" He asked me the typical question. I nodded.

"How often do you come back to visit?"

I replied, "Every two or three years."

"Do you see how fast things change here? Soon, Thu Thiem will be the new Hong Kong or Manhattan. You will see." He pointed to a large square block being dug up for an underground parking lot.

"The cost of living has risen so much here recently. Inflation is the highest in all Asia—more than twenty percent a year! A hundred dollars doesn't go far any more. A bowl of *Phở* costs two dollars already. A factory worker in Saigon only makes two dollars a day. I don't know how they pay for rent, eat, and still send money home to their family in the villages. They never go out; many share the same room and take turns sleeping because there are not enough beds to go around." He was on a roll now so I let him talk. He was working for his tip.

"Taxi drivers like me are a little better off than the factory workers, but not much. I barely make enough to feed a family of four. We live with our parents because we can't afford to move out on our own. Lucky for me, when my parents die, we will have their house. Not that I want them to die. I am just saying I am lucky I am their only son."

The way he talked reminded me of a boatman I had met on the river who showed me the island three years earlier before the tunnel was dug. I met that boatman on a hot, humid day in Saigon when I had run out of new things to see and do. My nephew and niece were playing tour guides for me, and they came up with a brilliant idea: "Let's go to Thu Thiem. It is only a boat trip, and for twenty dollars, we can cool off for a while on the water. Afterward, we can go find something to eat."

A few red and blue wooden boats were waiting for tourists at the riverbank. They had been built to carry vegetables, pigs, and chickens and shuttle villagers between the island and the city. Now with tourist money to be made, some became water taxis taking visitors on sight-seeing trips.

We got on a boat and the driver pushed off. He grinned as he recognized me as a Việt Kiều traveling with two young natives. Việt Kiềus are easy to spot. We look well fed, a bit fair skinned, and we carry a sense of being lost, not sure where we are at any time. I sized him up too, a man my age, maybe, but he looked much older. Unlike me—an office worker—he had lived on the river, worked on the river, and all that he owned fit in the boat.

The noise of the motor and the rich exhaust lulled me into another world. The brown silty water parted gently, pushing the water hyacinths and foam cups away. Plastic bags, feces, and dead matter like chicken guts littered the otherwise majestic river. The hint of raw sewage wafted in the steamy air. I shuddered to think that thirty years before, my friends and I swam in that water on hot days after class. It would kill me now if I happened to fall in—bacterial death would be slow and painful.

After laboring its way across the current to the other side of the river, the boat entered another time zone: the island belonged to another century. A wide barrier of dwarf palms grew out of the muddy bank. They bore heavy bunches of brown woody fruits the size of big clam shells loaded with clear and soft sweetness inside that local people used to make brown sugar and molasses. Beyond the border of palm trees were farm houses, simple but practical, built with local timber, woven bamboo for walls and palm fronds for roofs.

"This is my village." The boatman pointed at the huts. "I was born here, grew up here, a true Thu Thiem local. People farm and fish, and they go to Saigon to sell fruits, vegetables, fish, pigs and chickens. We have lived like that for many many years."

"What happened to the fish?" I asked him, looking at the dirty water.

He pointed at the curves in the shoreline where water flowed around tree trunks and sharp bends, "We used to fish there for large catfish, perch, and shrimp—very big tiger shrimp. They were here, everywhere. We could catch them with a dip net, easy catch. But not anymore."

He went on to talk about the factory discharge that killed off the underwater plants that the shrimp ate, and the fish died without shrimp to eat. Siltation from the upstream developments wiped out all of river life except the tough water hyacinth and the morning glory that thrived regardless.

As he talked, I studied his face. He had the brown leathery skin of a native adapted to the harsh Saigon sun and rain. His right eye was alert, but the left eye, just white jelly. His right hand gripped the accelerator and his bare feet pushed and pulled the rudder with minor adjustments. The stench of oily gasoline blended with the monotonous beat of the motor made my head throb.

Occasionally, the boat rounded another nook or cranny of the island's shoreline to reveal a small enclave of makeshift houses built on wooden stilts, clad with strips of rusty metal and scrap timber. Flimsy monkey bridges connected land to toilets that hovered perilously over water.

He pointed at the settlements, "These landless people came after the war. They had no place to go, lost their homes in the cities, and didn't want to go to the new economic zones for fear of scorpions and snakes. They came here instead. Here is a dead end. Nobody cares if you live or die."

They could be my family. My mother and brothers were forced to leave Saigon for the new economic zone of Tay Ninh after my father was sent up north to a labor camp for his crime of being in the South Vietnam army. It took them twenty years to finally make a living as farmers. Many people in the same situation never could and went back to Saigon and lived "underground" without permission. Some went to worse places, such as this.

"All my life I've been a boatman," he said. "I was born to fish, farm and drive boats."

He paused to remove the water hyacinths that had been wrapping around the propeller.

"We were the original boat people." He said sarcastically. "Actually, many became boat people after the war. I have a brother in Texas now. When people were leaving Saigon in 1975, he saw large ships leaving port, and everybody was fighting to get on board so he followed them. He had no idea what he was doing, but he went with the refugees to Guam and then a Baptist Church in Texas sponsored him. He went to Houston, got in fights with people in church and left for the Gulf to work with the shrimpers. Now he owns a shrimp boat and fishes the waters there. He writes once in a while about the shrimping business and how the Vietnamese have taken it over."

"How come you don't join your brother? Do you want to?"

He shook his head, "I don't speak English. I can hardly write in Vietnamese—neither can my brother. I don't know how he can live in a foreign country without being able to read or write. Maybe his children will do better. But for him, shrimping and fishing is all he knows. I am going to stay here with the river and the village. It is my life and my fate as a Thu Thiem local."

Then he pointed out to me the square gigantic metal structure on the bank. "You are looking at the future. The tunnel will be completed in a few years. Saigon is too crowded now so people will come here to live. There will be shops, markets, high-rises, roads, schools." He said with a vague sadness in his voice.

"What will happen to you?"

"I survive," he said. "All my friends are gone and dead. I am alone now on this river, me and my boat. This is my world and I can't imagine doing anything else. What can an illiterate half blind man do other than driving a boat? I see changes all around me, but I can't change with them. You have and you will because you can. I can't."

"Tell me about your friends," I asked, thinking about some of mine who died in the war right after high school. A few went overseas like me. Many stayed and survived like fish in dirty water: they couldn't stand it, but they adapted to the new corruption and ruthlessness.

"I don't know," he said. "They left me one by one. Some left the way my brother did and are probably living in America. They came back to visit Thu Thiem once in a while and then they stopped coming back. There is nothing here for anyone to miss. I lost some friends in the war, not the Vietnam war but the one after 1975. They went to Cambodia and died there."

He looked at me with his good eye and tried to guess my age. I told him I left the country on a scholarship before the war ended. I didn't experience how bad life was for those left behind, not first-hand anyway. He told me I was a special one and the gods took care of me because I had done many good deeds in a previous life, either that or my parents and grandparents were very kind and the kindness paved the way for me to be so lucky.

"I turned eighteen when the Vietnam war ended," he continued. "The North called it Giải Phóng for the liberation of the South but we still call it the Fall of Saigon."

"Many of my friends went to Cambodia." He frowned and took his time to resume. "We were forced to go fight there—everyone between eighteen and twenty-five. They trained us for three weeks, gave us rifles, and off we went. All the kids in Thu Thiem went, no exceptions. Some came back without legs, without arms, without heads. Many never came back at all. After my other brothers went, I was the only one left to take care of my mother. She was too old and tired to work in the garden to grow vegetables. She had only me so if I went, she would die."

"One night, I made up my mind. I sat by the kerosene lamp and sharpened a bamboo chopstick. I heated the sharp point over the flame and then placed it on my left eye. With a violent nod, I poked a hole in it and I passed out from the pain. With only one good eye left, I didn't have to go to Cambodia. It is better blind than dead."

"You are very kind," he gripped my hand with both of his. "Nobody ever wanted to know my story." We didn't talk much after that. I gave him a twenty-dollar tip when he dropped us off at the river bank.

After a quick drive around the island, I turned to look again at the island's skyline which began to resemble a smaller Hong Kong. "How do you like those towers?" The taxi driver asked, pointing at the twenty-story condominium buildings. The developed part of the island looked just like Singapore: clean, well planned, and expensive.

"The global recession doesn't seem to matter here. A new high-rise goes up every month. The government buys the land from the farmers at rock-bottom prices, squeezes them out if they don't move, and turns around to sell it to developers, foreigners. Government officials make obscene money. They drive Mercedes, buy private airplanes, and send their kids to America. The workers and the landless people suffer."

Before leaving the island, I turned to take one last look at Thu Thiem. Half of it had already been transformed. The other half would soon follow. In a short time, there would not be any more thatched houses. The flimsy toilets on the water would be replaced with speed boats docked along piers and marinas. The island would be lit up like Paris by night in the middle of the Saigon River. People would come from all over the world and pay two hundred dollars a day at the Marriott, eat banquets in fine restaurants served by half-clad young women, drink Tiger beer, and gamble in casinos.

Where had the boatman gone and what had happened to him? Maybe out there on the river, the one-eyed boatman had found his niche in the changing city. With his land gone, his mother dead, and a wooden boat with everything he owned, had he gone downstream to another city where life was slower? Had he gone upstream where the water was a bit cleaner? Had he become like the shrimp in this river that no longer sustained life?

"Where are you now?" I mumbled out the cab window.

The taxi driver dropped me off at my brother's place. "Here is the fare and a tip. Thank you for the trip. It was very nice."

"Thank you. How old are you? I can never tell with Việt Kiềus like you. You all seem much younger than you are."

"I am older than you think. However, I am very lucky." I replied.

Water Lily

In heavy makeup and high heels, she wiggled to adjust the tight little black dress. "I have to go to work now," my niece Liên said. "I have to pour drinks and serve hors d'oeuvres to Korean and Taiwanese customers. They tip in dollars." She turned to walk out the door and swung her bare leg over the back of a moped behind a helmeted man in black leather. She straddled the seat and grabbed his belly as they sped away into the smoky Ho Chi Minh City night.

Only a couple of hours ago, we were playing a board game of horse races with my nephew and his young wife. We rolled the dice and moved the cheap blue, red, yellow, and green plastic horses around the square paper board by the number of points the two dice rolled. Whoever could move all their horses into the barn fastest was declared winner. The loser had to eat ten bananas and I happened to love bananas. They ganged up on me and I ended up with a pile of banana peels while they rolled in laughter.

Liên sat modestly on the floor and carefully adjusted her summer dress to show just enough of her long legs. Her brother Ti was bare from the waist up. Tattoos ran down his right arm and right leg, some Maori, some his own designs. In this heat, a pair of shorts was the perfect way to walk around the house. I kept my tee-shirt on feeling conscious of my Việt Kiều's beer belly. Ti's wife's round belly announced a baby due in six weeks.

"Here are ten more bananas, Uncle Hao, hee hee hee!" Liên laughed with her head tilted back to let her black hair fall around her shoulders. "You can have all the bananas you want. These are the best tree-ripened ones—you don't have them in the US"

The bananas in Vietnam are firm and sweet since they are often picked the day before they hit the street markets. I'd forgotten that they used to be my favorite fruit. I dread the green bland bananas from Safeway that turn yellow with black dots. Then I have to gulp them down before they go soft all at the same time. Most often, I have to throw half of them out.

Then Liên got up and ran upstairs, "Sorry, Uncle Hao. I have to run. I have to work tonight." She disappeared for an hour and came down the spiral staircase in the little black dress. The house was awfully quiet after Liên left.

"Uncle Hao, let me show you Kendo." Ti pulled out two bamboo swords from a closet. "I have been practicing for a year now. I go to the dojo every other day. It keeps me focused." He pointed his weapon at my chin. "Here is how you hold the sword, your right-hand grips in front of the left. Keep your thumbs on top, little and ring fingers relaxed. Squeeze them when you strike to release maximum energy."

We stood facing each other with the tips of the split bamboo bundles barely touching. Then he slid the right foot forward, the left foot followed, and suddenly, he was within striking distance. "ZZZZEEE ZEE…" he hissed. I blinked. His bamboo blade came crashing down on my skull and stopped just an inch short of my forehead. He smiled, the smile I have loved since he was a baby.

"You see? You must always stare at your opponent in the eyes; advance without warning; shout as you deliver the blow; show no fear, ever." He showed it to me again, both arms raised over his head and then they came down with a straight sword cut. "I have practiced this move every day, thousands of times, the same strike every time. That's how they train in Kendo."

Kendo has become popular in Ho Chi Minh City. A famous Japanese teacher opened a dojo recently and attracted many youths to this sport. During my time more than four decades ago, it was judo. I grew up here in this city where my nephew and niece live now with my brother and his wife. The city had changed names from Saigon to Ho Chi Minh City. The country now has a post-war economy, a mad race to make money, an openness to the global market of ideas and products on the surface, and deep-rooted corruption as the foundation for big business. Liên and Ti are part of the forty million people born after the war. They are products of the new world here.

"Have a beer!" Ti stuck a cold one in my hand, grinning. "Happy Tết."

I had tried to return to this city every year when my mother was alive. She had lived through Giải Phóng and guided the family through the following ten years of hunger and the hardship made her sick and frail beyond her age. When I finally could return to see her after twenty years of being away, she was already suffering from a chronic illness without proper diagnosis and medical help but at least, I was able to see her off and on during the last seven years of her life. Now that she was gone, I spent most of my time with Liên and Ti, who showed me around the city and took me to restaurants, the ones that were not closed over the Tết holiday.

The other day, Liên donned her best Áo Dài and took me to the Nguyen Hue Street flower show. The one-mile street stretching from City Hall to Ben Thanh market was closed off to traffic and became the largest display of flower arrangements. The government spared no expense for this annual event that attracted millions of Vietnamese and foreign tourists from all over the world. The show included replicas of a village farmhouse, a green rice paddy, a monkey bridge over a fish pond, and a fishing net hanging on long bamboo poles. Other sections display every kind of orchid, every kind of Mai flower, bonsais, and arrangements to celebrate the Year of the Dragon.

Liên was my model and did a great job. Many serious photographers hired models for the day to pose for them. No matter how good you are as a photographer, pictures without pretty women in them are often just plain boring. I now have a collection of Liên in front of the huge straw dragon, among the orchids, next to the rice field. Her flowing red dress against the yellow Mai flowers in front of City Hall was calendar perfect. Other Việt Kiều eyed me with jealousy. "Where did you get such a gorgeous model?" The more polite Westerners paused to give compliments to Liên. "What a beautiful Áo Dài you have."

"I learned to pose in tourism school," she explained. "I learned to organize events for foreign visitors, set up banquets, and make speeches. I took many trips around the country to see all the famous destinations, but I also learned to look good, wear makeup, and walk around in pretty clothes."

Tourism is a booming industry fueled by new money and sustained by young women who learn their trades in tourism schools. One year or two of schooling and they are out hustling for tip money. I shudder.

"Liên has no talents," my brother Hiep poured me a shot of whiskey. Hiep is brother number five in the line of seven. "Not like Ti who is tough and intelligent, she is just pretty. She is not better than anyone else in any field. I don't know what to do for her."

Liên takes after her mother who was a tall and bosomy girl and kept Hiep from leaving Vietnam with my other brothers in a leaky boat, a decision that he may now regret. When I sent money home to pay for their escape, Hiep refused to go. He broke down crying because he could not leave without her and she could not leave without her family.

I watched Liên and Ti grow up in time-lapse—bit by bit— when I visited every year or every other year. In my mind as well as in my photo collections, I have earlier images of Ti swimming in a canal near the farm in Tay Ninh and I think of the leeches that got into my butt crack that day. Liên was smiling without her front teeth, a red hibiscus flower in her hair. Even as a five-year old, she already knew how to model.

Then there are pictures of Ti in a white shirt, blue shorts, and a blue bandana ready for school. I used to walk him to his middle school that was not far from the girls' high school, so I could snap pictures of the girls in the street in their white Áo Dàis like a flock of egrets in a rice field.

Ti and I have always been buddies. People take us for father and son since we have the same build, same height, and we laugh at the same jokes. However, he is far tougher than I who have spent most of my adult life overseas in lawful countries. He lives among twenty million people in Ho Chi Minh City, breathes the rich exhausts from millions of mopeds and diesel trucks, bribes his way through every process that involves paperwork, and earns respect from his friends by being just a little bit better than they are in every way.

"Let me show you the new apps I am developing for the iPad." Ti opened his new Apple gadget and moved his fingers on the glossy screen with the dexterity of a classical guitarist. "Here is the prototype of a game I am developing." Colorful balls shot up and fell down in various ways depending on the way he flicks his fingers. They exploded upon impact with targets that appeared randomly. "And here is another app for music lovers. The user can play notes, scales, modes, for the bass guitar, chords, you name it." He beamed.

I don't know how or where he learns to develop games and apps because he is mainly a self-taught guy. He had taken a few courses in college for a degree he did not complete. How he got to be this good is beyond me! His apps generate passive income that comes from advertisements based on how much the apps are used and it helps him spend time developing new apps.

"I am hiring a marketing company in the US to work for me," He said proudly. Who would have thought a Vietnamese kid would be hiring workers in the US?

"Now I have to work harder because the baby is coming. Next time you come back, the boy will be one or two years old. I bet he will look like me, and of course like you."

The dogs barked loudly, announcing someone was at the door. They stopped as soon as Liên stepped in with the high-heel shoes dangling in her hands and she wiggled her toes as she walked barefoot into the house. "Hello Uncle Hao, how are you doing? Are you bored yet?" She asked quietly. Her makeup ran a bit and her breath smelled like a mix of lipstick and beer.

"I had a rough night," Liên said. "These customers are mean. They didn't tip much and they grabbed a lot. Their hands went all over my legs and breasts. I must go shower." She ran up the spiral staircase.

"Uncle Hao, I keep telling Liên to get another job, but she likes the company and the tips," Ti said. "She is like a fish in dirty water. One day it is going to kill her."

"Can I offer you a drink?" he asked. "My father has a collection of cognac which he never touches. Let's celebrate Tết." He poured me a small amber drink in a shot glass. I sipped it slowly. It tasted hot and hard and sweet and bitter—all at once.

Liên came down again, her hair wet, and she had changed into pajamas. She smiled, "Uncle Hao, let's play another game of horse race." That's the only game I have played with her every time I visit.

"Aren't you tired?" I asked.

"No, I want to spend time with you now. You are not here for long—one week and you are gone. You are going to miss my twenty-first birthday. There will be a big party for me with all my friends. I wish you could stay."

"I have to go back to work. There is no Tết in America so they expect me there." I looked at her glistening eyes.

The four of us, Ti and his wife, Liên, and I played another game of horse race.

"Hey! You're cheating, Uncle Hao." Liên caught me at my regular tricks that I know she knew and yet every time it brought peals of laughter. Her laugh had changed over time and now it sounded like bells ringing with a bit of a throaty trill—a cat's purr. I counted the dice wrong, took a wrong turn, or went twice in a row on purpose just to let her catch me. Ti did the same but with a straight face and he got away with it unless his wife caught on and slapped him on the leg. We all laughed.

After we ate another bunch of bananas, Ti and his wife went to their bedroom. Liên invited me to the roof-top terrace to get some air. The house has a very small footprint in this crowded city but my brother had been able to add more floors and more rooms to accommodate his expanding family. Kids are always welcome to stay, get married and have more kids in the same house—no issues there.

The city had slowed its pace and the traffic was dying down. A yellow glow from street lights reflected off the low hanging haze and moist air. A light breeze cooled off everything. We sat among the fluttering clothes hanging on clotheslines and stared into nothingness.

Liên leaned on my shoulder with her soap-smelling silky hair. "Uncle Hao, please let me sit with you for a while," she whispered.

"Uncle Hao, are you happy?" I was surprised she asked that.

"I am okay. I am healthy, I work and travel, I see the world—no complaints."

"I mean happy happy. I worry about you. You always take care of other people but are you taking care of yourself?"

"I worry more about you, Liên. You are growing up so fast and I don't know how to help you."

"Uncle Hao, I am not a kid anymore. I wish I were still a little girl with a red hibiscus in my hair and you would roughhouse with me all day long. I miss that."

"Do you have a plan for what to do with your life? A boyfriend? Marriage? Kids?"

"No, I don't want to be like my parents, who work and work and never talk. I don't want to be responsible for someone else and resent him for making me unhappy."

I was amazed that she had figured it out at this early age. She had already become as jaded as I am.

Even near midnight, the neighborhood was still wide awake. Laughter and loud talking reverberated around the small alleys leading to our house. People were still playing cards, telling jokes, and singing karaoke. The comforting smoke of burning incense and cooked fish sauce permeated the midnight air. People refused to accept the night, especially those few nights of Tết when there is no work to do, time to catch up with friends and family.

Liên put her hand on mine, "See? You and I have the same hands, same size, same shape— amazing that even our fingers look alike." I agreed with her.

"I worry about you, a lot." I often thought about bringing her to America but as an uncle, U.S. immigration law doesn't let me. Besides, who am I to think that I can make anyone happy with what I do for them.

"Don't worry, Uncle Hao, I am a big girl now. I can take care of myself. I have many friends, and we take care of each other. I hope someday I will fall in love with a nice one, but all my friends are just friends for now."

"You will know when the time comes. Your heart will tell you." This I knew from experience.

"This is a dirty world I am living in, Uncle Hao. People buy and sell sex, drugs, and alcohol. They make money every way possible. Some are so rich you can't believe. They buy high-rise buildings, resorts, Rolls Royces, even airplanes. The money they tip us is spare change. They throw it around to amuse themselves while they drink cognac and smoke cigars, dealing business at the same time with foreigners. I am only picking up the scraps, I know, but it sure beats working in factories for two dollars a day."

"What can I do for you?"

"Nothing, Uncle Hao. I don't want you to worry. One day I will save enough money and come see you in the States. One day you will come here and attend my wedding."

She lifted her face and planted a kiss on my cheek. "I love you Uncle Hao, good night now."

She turned and ran down the steps to her room. I still smell the clean fresh soap in her blacky silky hair. I imagine a red hibiscus flower there where it always was when she smiled at me. I think of her name, Liên, water lily. I hope that she will live with her gift: a water lily rises above the dirty pond, its petals pure white, its core creamy gold, and its fragrance sweet, not a hint of mud.

One Ounce of Gold

I had first known of my younger brothers' intention to escape
Vietnam when I received a letter from my mother: "Your brothers
want to leave the farm and go live with Uncle Minh in the central
highlands." We had no Uncle Minh who lived in the highlands;
we didn't even have an Uncle Minh!

I wrote back: "I hope they will make it to the highlands. It is
colder, but they can grow many vegetables there. I will send some
money to pay for the long journey."

Since I got news of my brothers going to the central highlands to live with Uncle Minh, I opened my mailbox many times
every day, anxious for news. Nothing came from my mother for
about six months and then finally a letter, "Uncle Minh died, so
your brothers came back to the farm." *So, their plan to escape
failed.* I later found that the escapees got as far as the cape of Ca
Mau and the Viet Cong coast guard sprayed AK-47 bullets at their
boat. They jumped in the river and swam like rats as the boat
sank. Somehow, they managed to stay alive and out of trouble for
a while, but I had no idea what they did for months to survive. I
stopped hoping to see any of them again.

And then, one day, another telegram came to my apartment from my oldest brother Hoành, "We are in Pilau Bidong, Malaysia. Please get us out." My oldest brother, his wife, and my kid brother had made it to a refugee camp after all. *How did they do it? They crossed an ocean and survived!* That day, I broke open a bottle of Jack Daniels that I had saved for a special occasion and drank a few shots. Usually, I never drank alone, but that whiskey went down smoothly.

They had joined a hundred refugees packed in a thirty-foot boat, all trusting their lives to various gods. In the darkness, they slipped out into the ocean. After two days, the old motor quit running. They didn't bother rowing because they did not know which way was better: north, south, or east? North, they might find Hong Kong; south, maybe Malaysia, the Philippines; east, God knows what. The U.S. had stopped picking up refugees after the first year following the fall of Saigon in 1975. They didn't expect to be rescued by anyone. The boat people just hoped their vessels would hold up long enough for the journey and hit land somewhere without them running into pirates in the Gulf of Thailand.

Their three-day trip turned into twelve days of drifting. Water and food ran out on the sixth day. They floated with the trade winds southward in the open sea. They prayed for other boats and wished to die quickly if pirates found them first. There was nothing to do but pray.

"After we ran out of fresh water and food," my brother explained, "people had to cook whatever was left, and everything was salty. Someone found a piece of moldy bread on the floor, and we shared it. I still remember how good it tasted."

At last, a large wooden boat approached them from behind like pirate ships usually do. Everyone braced themselves. The men on the large boat yelled loudly but my brother couldn't tell what they wanted. The refugees hunkered down waiting for the assault to begin. After a few minutes of a standoff, the seamen threw over a rope for the refugees to catch. They passed down plastic jugs of water and rice wrapped in banana leaves and then towed the refugees' boat to a small deserted island and cut it loose. Glad for being saved from sure death, the refugees thanked the fishermen with a few ounces of gold they had hidden in the motor.

My two brothers and other refugees ate bats, snails, and mud crabs. They collected fresh water dripping in caves. Within a few days, another boat arrived from the Red Cross and took them to Pulau Bidong, the refugee camp in Malaysia. My brothers lived with thousands of refugees on the beach of Pulau, waiting for me to sponsor them to come to the U.S.

At the time, I was a new immigrant in the U.S. I went to San Francisco City College during the day and worked as a dishwasher at the Vietnam France Restaurant at night. At the corner of Divisadero and Bush Street, the restaurant was a family-owned business that would seat about fifty customers at capacity and with about two or three turnovers each night; we served more than a hundred clients with delicious and inexpensive dinners. Vietnamese cuisine involves a lot of dishes: Large, small, sauce dishes, bowls, spoons, forks, and chopsticks. All had to be sorted. All had to be scraped and washed.

For about four hours each night, I stood at the large metal sink with a plastic scraper and pushed morsels of rice and leftovers into the garbage can. Then I squeezed the power sprayer to blast away the scraps before loading the dishes into plastic trays and shoving them in the stainless-steel industrial washer. My plastic apron was coated with the washing spray and the bleach ate away at my pants. The grease and chlorine soaked through my skin and hair, and I smelled of fish sauce all day and night.

When the dinner rush died down, the staff sat down around the table in the back. Mr. Nam usually saved me a dish that someone returned to the kitchen. Wrong order, something like that. A succulent piece of Duck l'Orange or Chicken Cordon Bleu. Always his trademark, he added a round ball of rice and a serving of stir fried shredded cabbage in garlic and scrambled eggs.

Mr. Nam lived alone, above the restaurant. He only came down to cook and went back up to sleep. The restaurant was open six days a week and closed on Tuesdays. He had no car and no friends. He had a family in France, but he didn't want to talk about them. I found that he knew a lot about whiskeys and French literature. He mentioned occasionally that he used to work for the last Prince Bao Dai of Vietnam before the last royal family were exiled to France. He helped me send letters and money to my family in Vietnam.

Sending letters to and from Vietnam back then was like smuggling drugs. It usually took about one week to get a letter to an acquaintance in France and another two to three weeks to forward it from Paris to Vietnam. Sometimes, letters didn't make their way there at all—they either got lost along the way or were opened and censored somewhere in a dark, damp office of the political police in Vietnam.

Sending money home then was even more difficult because there was no legitimate way. Because Vietnamese piasters were worthless at an inflation rate of over a hundred percent a year, rich people hoarded gold and tried to transfer their wealth to a foreign country where they would eventually go. Thus, a smuggling business was born. It worked like this: you give money to a gold merchant in America or France in dollars. They usually had connections and could navigate any corrupt government and underground markets. They told their relatives in Vietnam to deliver the gold to your family there—the result was a net flow of money out of Vietnam at great profits for the money dealers.

When he arrived at SFO, my brother's black hair had been sun-bleached into a reddish brown and his lean but muscular body could pass as a day laborer. However, his leathery skin, heavily calloused hands, and dirty fingernails could not hide the inherited fine bone structure—not meant for farm work. Our ancestors had spent years in classrooms and passed exams to become mandarins and government officials to avoid working in the field. My brother must have been the first one in a long family lineage who actually worked with his hands to feed himself.

He smiled self-consciously with a missing front tooth when he saw me waiting at SFO in my bright red knit shirt with a green alligator logo.

"Anh Hao! I am so happy to see you. I am so happy you are here. I am totally lost..." He shook like a wet bird when we embraced. He looked around, over his shoulder, left and right, spooked by all the bright airport lights, well-stocked gift shops and fast walking, well-dressed travelers.

"Do you have a cigarette?" he asked.

I shook my head no.

"I need a smoke fast, and I don't have any money."

On the drive back to my apartment, I stopped at a 7-Eleven and bought a pack of Marlboro, the red pack that he preferred.

Right in the parking lot, he broke off the filter, inhaled the first cigarette, and then lit another. He offered me one. I shook my head.

"In Vietnam, everyone smokes, even kids. I am addicted."

After the third cigarette, he relaxed and gave a half-smile conscious of his stained and decaying teeth. "Thank you for the smokes, the best I had in years. I smoked everything I could find, corn stover, tobacco smuggled in from Laos, very strong!"

Even after thirty years of living in the anti-smoking state of California, he still can't kick the habit. He would sneak out to the back of his house to avoid his wife and the girls. His daughters would make faces when they saw him smoke, "Yuk!" He tried the patch, cold turkey, and smokeless tobacco without success, but he has cut way down because of the rising cost of heavily taxed cigarettes.

"Cheers!" He shoved a cold Heineken in my hand as soon as I arrived at his home. I came to celebrate my kid brother's thirty years of living in America and his fifty-fifth birthday. His thick black hair had turned a shocking white because he had skipped coloring it for two weeks, but at least he still had all of it. Somehow, I did not inherit that gene on my mother's side. Some say stress did it, but I think living well could too.

He sat cross-legged comfortably on his threadbare brown corduroy couch with a beer in his hand, talking slowly in a low voice, "You know, I have lived here longer than in Vietnam."

"Me too," I nodded. "I've spent most of my adult life going to school, working, doing just about anything to make a living, fitting in, becoming American."

Watercolor and oil paintings of scenes from Vietnam decorated his walls. One was a papaya plant bearing large swollen fruits, a palette of green and yellow. Against the pale green background, the largest fruit was ripening like a woman's breast, heavy with milk. Next to the papaya painting was one with a rooster crowing, beak held high, his back arched in a fluid curve flowing into his shiny green tail feathers. A hen and her chicks kept their heads down, hammering the ground. She scratched for worms stirring up dry dust.

The painting I love the most is a large square of dark green, blue, gray, a mix of the darkest colors, somber like a funeral home. If one looks carefully in the lower right-hand corner, a small lance-shaped object, like a falling bamboo leaf, seems like the painter's errant stroke or an oversight, something that should not be there—something that was tossed about, totally lost in a stormy sea.

He had sold a number of paintings and kept some. I had helped him sell and even bought a few of his paintings when I knew he needed the money. I wanted to buy that dark painting, "The Boat," but I knew he would never sell it to anyone. Not even to me, and that's why I never asked. One day, I want his daughters to have it.

Without any formal education in arts, he turned out beautiful watercolors, black and white charcoal, pastel, even oil paintings; my brother has a true gift. He's also collected and played many musical instruments, from the harmonica to violin, all self-taught, but painting is his passion. At one time, he rented a stall at the San Jose flea market and did portraits for five bucks apiece. Then, after he got married, he put away his brushes and easel and applied for a regular job in a computer company as an engineer.

"I don't need much money for myself," he used to tell me. "I can live on very little and I could survive as an artist. Years of living in the new economic zone, I ate sweet potatoes and boiled leaves day in and day out. They are inexpensive and good for me." Eating very little meat is a habit that he maintains even today. He gave me long explanations about why he chose the potato diet, "People are originally starch eaters. If you don't eat greasy foods, your body doesn't have to work hard to digest, and you don't get sick." He tried to convince me to change to his minimalist lifestyle.

"So brother, tell me your plans, what are you going to do next?" I asked, just to get him to say something.

"I want to buy some land in Gilroy, an acre, maybe two. I want to start a farm," he squeezed his hands together, "I always love the land, the feel of clay and sand between my fingers and the brown worms that make the earth good. They are the real workers, you know?"

"How about Silicon Valley? Is there a management job for you?" I asked.

"There is not much for me here in the high-tech industry. I am getting too old to be competitive. Look around: Everyone my age is being laid off. The jobs are going overseas. The new hires are younger and cheaper and have to compete with bright kids from all over the world. Next stop is unemployment. Early retirement," he smiled ironically.

Then his eyes lit up.

"I was the only one in the village who could read, write, and do simple math. I had an important job: keeping track of supplies and rations for the cooperative. I was only sixteen but I had responsibilities over twenty families who trusted me. They even wanted me to marry their daughters. Imagine that!" he smiled.

"There was this street vendor who really liked me, I could tell. She used to sell rice porridge in the morning and sweet chè in the evening. I liked her too, but I was too shy to say anything, you know? I just didn't know what to say to girls. Of course, I couldn't tell anyone that I was planning to escape; I couldn't tell her either.

One night, as we sat in the dark watching the stars, she took my hand and placed it on her breasts and asked me if I found them soft. I didn't respond and she cried. I suppose by now, she would have been married to a farmer and had a bunch of kids."

He quickly changed the subject to the computer gadgets that he tested, the lay-offs in his company, his worries about the mortgage, and the two girls who grew up fast with needs for dental braces and designer jeans. He dismissed all his work and daily life activities as deadly boring, and the reason he worked at all was to provide for his wife and daughters.

"Brother, tell me the truth. After having lived and done so many things, what have been your best memories?" I asked.

After a short pause, he sighed, "I often think about Tay Ninh. We were hungry when our father was sent to a jungle camp up north and you were gone and I grew up in a hurry. Brother Hoành was also in re-education for his army service. Brother Bê went to Cambodia with the youth volunteer army. I became the oldest of the litter so kept Ma and our younger brothers alive for years with my own hands. I made decisions for the family and sometimes for the whole village. I learned by doing, changing a forest to a farm. I cut down trees, built a house, and dug canals to bring water from the river to the farm to grow rice and cassava. I learned to lead, by example, by sacrifice, by gaining people's trust and respect. I was a leader, you know?"

"What's different now?" I asked.

"Here in Silicon Valley, I am one of a few hundred thousand computer engineers, all with degrees from someplace. Sure, I rode the high-tech wave when I came here, but that wave has long passed. When I look around: most of us have been laid off. I am among those to go next."

"Oh, then another highlight of my life—you wouldn't believe it—was Pulau Bidong. I helped the illiterate folks with their paperwork, applications, and letters to their families in exchange for cigarettes. The Red Cross fed us mackerel, Spam, and canned beans. In the afternoon, I went swimming in the warm ocean. Camp Bidong had one of the most beautiful beaches in the world. I would love to see it again one day. What more do you want? Work, eat, and go to the beach! Better than starving in a stinking boat—better than testing electronic circuits every day."

"Why don't we do it one day, just you and me. We can go back to Vietnam together, go visit the farm, to the place where you set out to sea, to Pilau Bidong, just you and me?" I said.

"Brother, thank you for what you did for me."

I grunted something, knowing what he was going to say.

"Without you, there is no me," he continued. "Do you remember the ounce of gold?"

"No big deal, brother. I wish I could do more."

"It changed my life forever."

"I was fifteen years old when our father went to a re-education camp up north and mother had to sell all we had to feed us. That lasted about one year, and being desperate, we followed the government's order to leave our place in Saigon and go to Tay Ninh. They gave us a plot of forest to farm in the new economic zone. Ma needed me to be strong to do farm work. We lost touch with you for so many years before you found us again through Mr. Nam and his contacts in France."

"Then one day Ma made me go. She saw me read a book one evening by the kerosene lamp, a classic literature book that didn't get eaten by the termites. Something happened in her head and the next day she gave me the gold and told me to go. She said that being a farmer was not for me and I needed to go join you in America. I told her I wanted to stay, but she told me that my job was done there and the village would be fine without me."

"Brother Hoành and his wife had arranged for everything and they told me to join them with the escape plan. They told me to tell no one but our mother. The morning I left the village, I waited outside for the bus to get to the city. Little brother Hòa came out to see what I was doing and I hugged him for a long time. Somehow, he could tell that I was saying good-bye. He ran after the bus until he couldn't run any more. I saw him collapse in the red dust and diesel exhaust."

In 1980, gold was eight hundred and fifty dollars an ounce, an all-time high back then, perhaps because of all the smuggling to and from Vietnam. It was also the going price for a place on one of these refugee boats. I was still a student and a dishwasher in a small restaurant in San Francisco so I had no savings. I borrowed and scrounged enough for three ounces and Ma decided that one was to buy him a chance for a future. He became one of the boat people—hundreds of thousands who bought and stole their way out of the country in unsafe vessels, trusting their lives to the sea, tossed about like a bamboo leaf in a storm.

I often wonder about all the scenarios that could have happened to my brothers. What if they never came to America? What would happen to my sister-in-law if they were captured by the pirates? What if they drowned and died in the South China Sea and I spent the rest of my life regretting my role in this plot? What if I had done nothing?

I often think about what that ounce of gold had bought. It gave me so many years of having my kid brother with me and watching his daughters grow. I would willingly pay many times more than that for the privilege. I hope his life here has been fulfilling and sometimes I have my doubts but then who is to judge? My nieces have the opportunity to live their American dream. My brother and I can get together once in a while to share a beer and talk about where we came from. That alone is comforting enough for me.

"Coming here to America is really all about the next generation and the opportunities for the kids who are born here. We are a lost generation—you and me. We straddle the ocean. Our bodies are here but our thoughts are there. We are not whole, only halves." He stuck another cold Heineken in my hand.

Undocumented

It was a rainy night in San Francisco, dark and cold. I had just finished my work at the Vietnam France Restaurant on Divisadero Street and was heading home to the Sunset District. It was late and I was tired. My mind was wandering and confused. I had just received another letter from the Immigration and Naturalization Service: "Your petition is denied." Ma had written about my father and how worried she was about him and my brothers. He had been taken to a jungle camp up north and kept for four years already, and she had only been allowed to visit him once. She asked for fifty dollars to buy food. My brother Hoành also asked for help and lots of it, money that I didn't have. I had just given up my Colombo Plan scholarship in Australia because I didn't plan to return. I was staying in San Francisco with an expired tourist visa with my wife Diep. We lived between three countries and were citizens of none.

I was driving a lime green Chevy Vega that I had bought for five hundred bucks, the worst car ever made in America. It was tied with the Ford Pinto for that title, actually. Although the Pinto had been known to explode if hit from behind, the Vega won hands down with its oil-guzzling aluminum engine and a body held together by rust. Every time I stepped on the gas, it left a cloud of smoke with enough unburned hydrocarbons to trigger climate change. For my first car in America, it was alright, and I couldn't ask for more with my meager income. I was climbing up a hill on Geary Boulevard when red and blue lights flashed behind me.

My pants were still soaking wet from the dishwashing and my whole body reeked of fish sauce and chlorine. Now this.

"Show me your driver's license and registration," the well-armed patrol officer demanded.

"Officer, what did I do?" I asked, trying to be friendly. I have always had a phobia for people in uniform. It didn't matter what kind. Anybody with guns usually did more harm than good.

"Stay in the car. Just show me the papers."

I complied, reluctantly.

"You were doing fifty in a thirty-five zone." He was stern.

I swore I wasn't. He didn't believe me. The Vega was just not that fast up a hill; however, I knew not to argue with police officers. Just to get it over with.

"Do you have work papers?" He shone a flashlight in my face.

I didn't know what he meant. In fact, I didn't know if one needed any other papers to drive. I waited for him to elaborate, but he let that go and gave me a ticket. Thirty-five bucks. There went my earnings for the week.

At the end of each week, Cô Quỳnh, the restaurant owner, rounded up the staff and paid them. I got two twenty-dollar bills in a small yellow envelope. Sometimes, I was surprised to find an extra ten when the restaurant did well. She paid me a dollar fifty an hour for five hours each night. This was much lower than the minimum wage in the late 1970s, but I couldn't complain. She never asked me about any work papers, and I didn't have any. She was pleased that I was hardworking and reliable. There were only two of us in the kitchen, Mr. Nam and me. He single-handedly cooked all the meals for fifty diners at peak capacity. I was the dishwasher and sometimes assisted with chopping vegetables and slicing meats. After rush hour, he would give me a dinner plate, and we ate together. A shot of whiskey after dinner with him was good too.

Earlier in the day, I'd gone to UC Berkeley to talk to Dr. John Helms in the Department of Forestry. I found his office on the second floor of Mulford Hall. "Welcome to Forestry School," he said. I recognized his accent and he knew mine.

"So, you are from Australia, too?" I ventured.

He smiled. "From your application and transcripts, you have finished three years at the Australian National University Forestry School in Canberra. Good school. Excellent. Just one more year to go. Why didn't you finish?"

I explained my situation, leaving out the visa and the overstay. "Family reasons, we wanted to be near my wife's family."

"I understand," he smiled in a friendly Aussie way. "You can transfer all your credits here, but you have to complete the core requirements for the Berkeley curriculum and the last two years of the Forestry Program."

I knew that every school required all students to meet their core requirements. Besides, the knowledge of eucalyptus ecosystems I learned in Australia would be useless here. The blue gum trees introduced to the west coast are just a fire hazard as far as many Californians are concerned.

"We will accept you as a transfer student. No worries. You can register now and good luck!"

I went to Sproul Hall, excited about my easy acceptance into UC Berkeley, a cool place to complete my degree that I had set out to do when I left Vietnam a few years back.

A smiling lady accepted my paperwork and the reference from Dr. Helms. "Welcome to Berkeley. You are the first Vietnamese to be accepted to Forestry school here. Congratulations!" Ma would be proud to know. I was the first in my family to go college, and now to UC Berkeley.

"Are you in-state yet?" she asked.

"What do you mean?"

"Have you been a resident in California for at least one year?" she was about to sign off.

"Yes, I have been here more than one year, just," I answered firmly.

"Do you have your green card with you? We need to see it."

My heart sank. That's the question I dreaded most. Legal immigrants start their residency in the U.S. with a document called "green card." I didn't have it.

"I am sorry, I have a slight problem with my status. I am still waiting for approval from the Immigration Office," I tried to make it sound like an oversight, like I forgot to bring my wallet.

"That's OK. It just means that you have to pay out-of-state tuition, which is twice what residents pay. I am sorry about that. Once you have one-year residency from the date of the green card, you will be in-state."

It hit me hard. I would have to reduce my classes in half and take longer to finish the degree, but at least it was a hurdle and not a wall. I had run into the wall every time I applied for a job before I found one at the Vietnam France restaurant where I didn't need to explain about my status. Potential employers asked the same question: "Are you a citizen? A permanent resident?" and that was the end of the interview.

I had resorted to odd jobs from people who didn't ask questions and paid in cash. I always found some in the ads section of the newspaper. One was to deliver phone books for three weeks. It was like a paper route except the books were really heavy. I loaded them in a shopping cart and pushed them up and down the hilly sidewalks of San Francisco. I cleaned BBQ pits, mowed lawns, and stocked a tire warehouse. Back in Canberra, I had spent one summer working for the City Parks and Gardens department and another summer measuring trees in the Stromlo pine forest, so physical work didn't bother me one bit. The Vietnam France restaurant was the longest gig and lasted two years. A friend of my in-laws introduced me to the owner and Cô Quỳnh hired me right away. She never asked about the green card and I never said anything.

Diep and I had arrived in San Francisco on January 3, 1977, with full intention to return to Canberra. We were newlyweds. We'd gotten married one year ago and were students in Australia.

It turned out that we never used the return flight tickets. We traveled with temporary Certificates of Identity from Australia because we were not yet citizens Down Under, and our Vietnamese passports were worthless after the fall of Saigon. Australia had been very kind to us, and I breached the contract with them by leaving without completing the scholarship program. I was in love with the blue sky in Sydney the first summer, taking English classes with my cohorts in the morning and going to Bondi Beach in the afternoon. I enjoyed the view of Lake Burley Griffin from my dorm in Canberra and the fog hanging over the tall poplar trees. I still wish that I could somehow say a proper goodbye to the country that saved me from a life of poverty and possible death. They gave me a full scholarship and even a stipend to live on. Life was good for me back there and I had no reason to leave. Had I known what was to follow, I would certainly have hopped on the Qantas airplane to go back to Canberra as scheduled. But sometimes in life, you listen to your heart.

We were supposed to be in America for only one month as tourists. The reunion with my in-laws was bittersweet since it had been a year and a half without them in our lives. One evening after dinner in Chinatown, my father-in-law convinced us that Diep should be eligible to stay in the U.S. because the INS would allow her reunion with her parents, and I should too because we were married. He thought that we could apply for political asylum because we were basically Vietnamese refugees and Australia was only our temporary residence. Had we gone back to Australia then, they could have sponsored us, but it would take ten years. It sounded simple enough so we filed an application for asylum with the INS with much hope for an easy decision. Then we waited every day for approval of our applications. Six months later, our petition was rejected for the first time because we arrived in the U.S. from Australia and not a refugee camp.

Mr. Hoffman, an immigration lawyer of the USCC (United States Catholic Conference) on Market Street took our case for free. He was a passionate advocate for immigrants and had helped many from Mexico and Central America, all pro bono. He thought that we had a good case: we were refugees from Vietnam even though we were not entering from a camp in Malaysia, Hong Kong, or the Philippines. "What you need is amnesty," Mr. Hoffman said. "It means forgiveness because the INS doesn't know what to do with you. They can't deport you to Australia because you are not citizens there. It is inhumane to send you to Vietnam, of course. You are a special case, maybe the first for Vietnamese in America." I've made many firsts that I am proud of, but not this one.

It was comforting to know that we could not be deported, but we were still in limbo–application pending status. With that status, I could obtain a driver's license and a social security number for ID purposes, but I didn't have the most important document for a normal life: the green card. School tuition costs twice as much for non-residents. I could not get any legitimate job that required proof of permanent residency. The INS didn't care about our case because we were not their problem. We had already been undocumented for two years at this point, and this could go on forever.

"You are so unhappy. I am sorry, maybe you should have gone back to Australia," my mother-in-law said one night. "It's OK if you decide to return. Maybe they will take you back."

There was no turning back. Diep would be unhappy now that we had come so far for her to be near her folks. As their only daughter, she loved them and had a sense of duty that all Vietnamese children had been trained to bear. I would have done the same for my family. Of course, I couldn't go back alone. The only choice for me was to stay and wait for amnesty.

Diep was the most beautiful Vietnamese girl in Australia back in the day. She was like the princess in the kingdom and every Vietnamese man came from all over the country to vie for her attention. Of the three hundred and fifty Colombo Plan students that came to Australia over a decade, less than fifteen percent were female, so competition among the male Vietnamese students for a mate from the same culture was keen. Word got out that the counselor's daughter was a beauty, and her name Diep literally means white butterfly. All the boys knew her name and gladly made the trip to Canberra to visit the embassy for any business reason and to catch a glimpse of the butterfly princess. I was mildly interested, but I was preoccupied with studying and helping my family with everything I could. On Christmas of 1974, all the Vietnamese students and residents in Canberra were invited to the embassy for a party and I went too. I wore my best clothes, a white shirt, polyester tie and the dark blue suit jacket that Ba gave me the day I left Saigon. It had been the only suit he owned and he had it made to order back in the day when he married Ma. Always uncomfortable in crowds, I stayed back in a corner, watching the boys converge on Diep like hungry diners at a buffet table. In her elegant green *Áo Dài*, she was the center of attention. She fielded the incoming attacks with the ease of an Aikido black belt. One opponent after another fell by the side, but they kept coming back for more. Suddenly, her father pulled me in and introduced me to her, "Look, Diep, Anh Hao is a forestry student at the Uni. Maybe you can ask him questions about the school." So, I had a way to cut in line. I found out that she was going to the same university, majoring in linguistics so that she would one day be an ambassador for South Vietnam. We talked for a few minutes. I mainly answered questions she asked, then I yielded time for others to give their best shots.

Before I left the party, I saw Diep engaged in a long talk with Anh Hanh, another Colombo Plan student, one year my senior. He had moved up to the top of the buffet line and held his position. Hanh was also a Forestry student with a macho reputation even among the Aussies, mostly for the copious consumption of beer. He was a handsome and well-dressed guy who knew how to charm the ladies and was always surrounded by admirers for his soccer prowess. She seemed attentive and he was animated, going for the goal. I figured that was a done deal. Nobody could compete with Mr. Hanh.

On the way back to the dorm, I found myself alone in the city. I rode my bike in the foggy darkness with no other soul on the road. Canberra was a small city where most people worked for the government, the university, and the embassies. There was no other reason to be there. All my friends feared being sent to the Uni in Canberra. A joke circulated that Canberra was the aboriginal word for the place between the two breasts—there is nothing to see there.

My friends preferred life in Sydney, where we were all together the first summer. Melbourne was also a fine choice. Adelaide and Brisbane were acceptable, but Canberra was like banishment to the outback. As the capital, it was a completely planned city in the middle of nowhere to settle the rivalry between Sydney and Melbourne. Blazing hot in the summer and freezing cold in the winter, it resembled a huge green park: wide streets lined with eucalyptus, London plane, elm, and street trees from all over the world, and very sparsely populated. A city of straight lines designed by an architect and built by engineers. A few random cars in the streets reminded me that I wasn't wandering in the post-apocalypse, but I'd see no humans, no sounds, no life. At night, Canberra was a ghost town. I felt like an alien who had just landed from Neptune, so out of place and so far away from home.

I had already forgotten about the embassy party, but a few days later, somebody knocked on my dorm room door and said I had a phone call. Diep was on the line, asking for me. She inquired if I'd had a good time and I simply answered that it was a nice event. I thought she was doing a survey for the embassy and perhaps fundraising for a charity in Vietnam. She remembered that I have six brothers. I didn't mention Anh Hanh, and neither did she.

Suddenly, she asked, "Do you want to come to my house for lunch this Sunday?"

Of course, I said yes and a few days later I rode my old Yamaha bike to her house in the suburb of Queanbeyan early in the morning. I rang the bell and expected her father to appear with a gun in his hands. In addition to people in uniform, I was deadly afraid of people in high office. Her father was the counselor at the embassy, and we students came with hat in hand to renew our passports every year to be allowed our continued stay in Australia. My livelihood was on the line. Her father opened the door in his pajamas and asked, "Who is there?" I identified myself and said I was sorry I didn't know what time I should be there, so I came as early as I could. He let me in. The house was small and sparsely furnished, not what I expected of a diplomat's residence. "I am just a civil servant for South Vietnam," he seemed to have read my mind. He sat me down on the light-framed Danish teak sofa and talked to me about my studies. He wanted to know more about the Colombo Plan and his responsibility to take care of the students. I suspected that the embassy needed to monitor students and made sure to know of any subversive activity. And then he switched to the topic of classical music. "Bach was inspirational, but an hour of Segovia playing Bach will put you to sleep." Then he did the most amazing thing: he pulled out from a hard case a Spanish guitar that he brought from Madrid. "We owe Andres Segovia a huge favor," he tuned the guitar by ear. "He single-handedly brought the guitar to the concert stage and made it a respectable instrument but he also removed all the Flamenco out of the music because he said it's the music of the streets." I didn't know anything about classical or Flamenco music, but I fell in love with the sound of that guitar. He started with the Spanish ballad Romance Antiquo with its beautiful melody. "See? Very sweet, very classical." Then he switched to Soleares and Alegrias full of sadness and joy and explained Flamenco music to me. Music was his passion and he had studied the classical guitar as well as Flamenco while working for the embassy in London.

He had been in the diplomatic corps for years and held many posts alternating two years overseas and two years in Saigon. This was his tour in Australia. Diep's family belonged to the aristocrats of Vietnam. We would never have met in Vietnam because our worlds would never come together. My father and mother had no artistic pursuit at all; they toiled to give us food and shelter and never talked to us about anything other than doing school homework. Diep's mom cooked Bun Bo Hue, my favorite noodle soup, for lunch. She used spaghetti noodle to substitute for the rice noodle that was not available in Canberra back then but the rest of the soup with lemongrass, pork neck bones, and slices of beef in a red-hot chili broth was authentic Hue, my father's birthplace. At the table, the conversation was lively; they discussed the situation in Vietnam, the prospect of what would happen now with the U.S. devolvement, and news of another imminent invasion of the South. I dropped a piece of bone on the floor and wondered if I should pick it up. Everyone pretended they didn't see that.

Diep still laughs every time she mentions the dropped bone. Sometimes, she tells me that she was moved by my loneliness: "When I first met you, I saw the saddest boy. I had many suitors who tried to impress me. You didn't even bother." In Canberra, I was really happy for a change, truly happy to have a companion, and a beautiful one as well. We met daily on the campus library lawn among the white birch trees. I shared with her a ham and cheese sandwich, an apple and one boiled egg I packed for lunch. We talked and talked.

Diep had many interests that I had never known. She loved foods and specialties from different countries and read famous books in English, French, and Spanish. She loved music and even played the piano. She knew all the names of actors and actresses and the year each movie came out. She could remember people's names and birthdays, including all members of my family. It was like the sun had shone a light into the corner of my small room with only a window overlooking the past.

I had very limited experience of the world back then. All my life, I had hardly gone out to restaurants or movie theaters. My friends and I only went to two local movie theaters, one with Indian movies with constant singing and dancing, and the other with Chinese Kungfu that featured non-stop fighting with the same sound effects and yelling in dubbed Vietnamese. I learned to enjoy going to the university Cinathons with all-night movies and we sat holding hands the whole time. My college friends even teased us about being the Vietnamese Romeo and Juliet. "You look like a couple of dolls," they teased. With my student's stipend, I could only take her out once a month to her favorite little joint "Gus" in the Civic Center. We shared one order of her favorite beef steak and an apple strudel for dessert. Other times, we had Hawaiian-style pizza with lots of ham and pineapple, and my gastronomic world opened up by following her tastes.

Four months after our meeting at the Christmas party at the embassy, Saigon fell as we helplessly watched from afar. Since the 1972 Paris agreement that President Nixon negotiated with

China, South Vietnam was abandoned by the U.S. Triggered by Watergate and Nixon's resignation in 1974, North Vietnam initiated the invasion of the South. Those who had money had started to move their wealth overseas so they could soon follow. Watching the collapse of our homeland was like seeing a cancer patient die. We received news of defeat one city at a time as the North marched South. We read about the siege of Tan San Nhat airport to drive the last Americans out of Vietnam and saw photos of tanks rolling onto the lawn of the Independence Palace to put an end to South Vietnam and begin Giải Phóng. April 30, 1975 marked the day the people of South Vietnam prepared for the bloodbath that would follow. The embassy of South Vietnam in Canberra was no longer recognized. The Colombo Students were afraid of being sent home, but our Australian sponsors were gracious to assure us that we could remain where we were without changes in their support.

Soon after, Diep's parents started packing to go to the U.S., where they had always wanted to live. They got visas to enter the U.S. as refugees since they were diplomats of South Vietnam, and there was an open window for them to immigrate legally.

On the lawn of the library, between the birch trees that were shedding their yellow leaves, Diep broke the news, "I am losing you. I have to leave Australia and you behind. My parents are going to San Francisco, and I am supposed to go with them."

I was still a student, barely twenty years old. I had no money, no job, no plans. I was living off the largess of the Australian government with tuition and a stipend that paid for the dorm room. I had nothing to offer her.

"Maybe I will visit you when I graduate," I promised. "I will save money and come visit you in America."

"It will be a long time," She started crying. "At least three more years."

The next day, we met on the library lawn, and she had stopped crying. "I will stay here with you if we get married." She made me promise that we would get engaged before her parents left. I was so happy she decided to stay with me.

We said goodbye to her parents when they boarded the plane leaving for America. "Goodbye, my dear parents," I said. Since the first lunch at their house, I had been there every Sunday and we often watched the news together. I had talked to them more than I had ever talked to my own parents and I had adopted them as my own. "We will join you someday when we graduate from college." I had no idea when, I had no idea how. The end of that year we got married.

"It must have been the cheapest wedding ever," Diep still teases me sometimes. "Let's get married again properly." It was just the two of us with a couple of witnesses and blessed by the Pastor of the CMA Church. Before the wedding, I bought her a ring with the smallest diamond when we got engaged and we went to Sydney to buy a wedding dress. It was just a plain white dress and a big white hat. I had bought a gray suit and a red velvet bow tie from Selvitex Menswear in Canberra where I moonlighted as an assistant salesman. Selvitex had the corniest slogan: "It is a bagga fruit, it's a Selvitex suit." No wonder the company quickly went out of business. After the short ceremony at church, the eight of us went to the only Vietnamese restaurant in Canberra, owned by an ex-employee of the embassy. They gave us the best meal and refused payment. "Your dad was the best boss I ever had," the owner said about Diep's father.

Sometimes, I still feel bad about how poorly I took care of

Diep during the first few years of our marriage, and think I may have traumatized her for life. That was the time that we should have been most happy, being newlyweds, but we were not. I worked and worried too much and spent all our savings to help Ma and my brothers. I denied her the little luxuries that couples should enjoy, a nice trip, dining out, and gifts. We shopped at St Vincent De Paul. She had postponed her education indefinitely and abandoned her plan to become a diplomat. Thank goodness we were young and healthy enough that we didn't need much medical or dental care.

One day, we walked through the Tenderloin district and stopped by St. Anthony's Catholic Church. Along a rundown street in a seedy neighborhood, a line looped around the block at noon hours, people waited to be fed at the soup kitchen. One bearded man told us, "Come on, it's not bad." We looked for the sign "Clinic" and waited for our turn to see a doctor or someone with credentials.

"You are young and healthy. What do you need?" the doctor asked.

"We need birth control pills. Can you help us with a prescription?" I looked at my feet.

He stood up, "Sorry, this is a Catholic organization. We can't help you."

We kept walking toward Market Street. It was time again to check in with Mr. Hoffman.

The front desk said that he was in, but he would not see anyone, too busy that day.

"We just need a minute with him," I pleaded.

"He is preparing for court and shouldn't be interrupted." She continued typing.

We waited in the lobby. I don't know why we sat there for hours but we had no other plan. We had to beg for help to get that green card. That was all I was thinking about, every breathing moment.

Finally, Mr. Hoffman emerged from his office on his way to the bathroom and we ambushed him. He looked at us sympathetically and shook his head, "No news. We have to wait for the INS to respond and they respond every six months. Nothing I can do."

I finally graduated from UC Berkeley with a degree in Forestry. It took a while for me to complete the core requirements, but I made it. Right away, I applied for a job with Weyerhaeuser Company in Washington State. I had worked as a student intern with them the summer before and they liked what I did for the R&D division. Diep and I loved the Tacoma Seattle area, green and peaceful forests of tall Douglas fir around communities of wooden houses. We loved the lakes and fresh seafood from the Puget Sound. God's country. We had wanted to move there to live after I graduated.

They flew me to the Tech Center for an interview and tour of the entire research facility. I was among the top candidates, and they wanted to offer me a job. Mr. Aaron Hazard of the HR division went through the necessary steps to onboard me, and I hit the same wall when he asked the dreaded question. I assured Mr. Hazard that it was a matter of time, my petition was pending and I was not illegal, I was only in limbo. That didn't pass the test. "Please apply again when you get the green card. I am sorry I didn't check sooner. We are wasting our time." Mr. Hazard ushered me to the door.

Diep paid dearly, too, for the decision we made. She had postponed her college education and even given up her pursuit of linguistics: "It is not practical," she said. "I don't have a country to represent anymore. The hospitals always need nurses, and they pay well." She completed a certificate at a community college to be a nurse's aide. She signed up with a registry, which sent her to many different places depending on her needs, but Franklin Hospital had the most cases. Lucky for us, sometimes they didn't require proof of residency, and because of the nursing shortage the registry took her without questions. She was among the first to witness the AIDS outbreak in the Castro Street area. "Young men. They came in and died. Maybe this is my true calling: I am easing the pain and suffering for society." She showed no fear of the mysterious illness.

In the Sunset District of San Francisco, Diep and I shared a two-bedroom apartment with her parents and her teenage brother, and he had to sleep in a corner of the living room. It was a bit crowded there, but we had no choice. We avoided the neighbors and the landlord because we violated the rental agreement with more residents than allowed. My in-laws lied to them that we were visitors only, not staying long. We paid part of the rent with the money I made working for Vietnam France Restaurant and they subsidized us with food. My father-in-law still played the guitar in his pajamas and my mother-in-law cooked Vietnamese food. They had lost their status as diplomats and started over from scratch, so we all lived on a tight budget. They treated me like their own child, but I felt entrapped. I ate what they cooked and spent my weekends the way they wanted, as they always included us. My father-in-law usually bought food in large quantities to save money and one time he must have had a month's supply of turkey legs. We ate dark turkey meat every day and amassed a pile of bones, each the size of a small child's femur. Sometimes the bones got stuck in the garbage chute, and I was afraid the neighbors might call the cops on us. In America, I had become a hostage in a small apartment and in the country that didn't welcome me.

It bothered me even worse when my friend Peter asked about our living with the in-laws. Peter was an older friend in Forestry at Berkeley, perhaps the only other married person in class. He lived with his wife in San Francisco, and we used to share rides from the city to school. Peter was curious why I didn't move out on my own. That's what adults do in America. I had no answer because I didn't want to tell him we were undocumented. That's the topic I didn't want to disclose to anyone, like a family shame, a subject for ridicule, as in many racist jokes that were really mean and not funny to me. I was not far off from picking lettuce and strawberries in Salinas had it not been for living with the in-laws. Not only was my manhood being questioned, I was slowly losing Diep. She had turned from being my wife to the daughter that she once was. Back in Canberra, we used to talk for hours about our future, our plans, and us. We had been a unit before, but now she turned to her parents for advice, and they didn't say: "Talk to your husband."

One day we made another desperate visit to Mr. Hoffman's office, and he gave us the good news: "Amnesty finally came. The INS had forgiven you for your trespassing." After five years of having no status, we became permanent residents with green cards. Around the same time, I sponsored Hoành, his wife, and my younger brother Ho from a refugee camp in Malaysia. They settled in San José and thrived. Ba was released after ten years in a labor camp, a broken man but alive. Diep and I could focus now on building our own lives.

To celebrate becoming U.S. citizens in 1985, Diep and I went out to a steakhouse for the first time in years. We ordered one T-bone steak and a big salad for both of us plus an apple strudel for dessert. They were the same items that she liked at Gus in Canberra. She preferred the meat around the bone and usually left it clean when she was through. "I was a dog in my previous life," she grinned.

I envied her ability to live in the moment. It didn't take much to make her happy, and good food usually did the trick.

"Did you regret coming to America?" She looked up from the dog bone. She had no problems saying whatever was on her mind. Unlike her, I was not usually expressive.

"No," I lied. Had I stayed in Australia, I would have become their citizen right away and may have been able to help my family more during the years they needed me the most.

"What about you?" I knew she had her losses too. She had given up her chance to complete her education and the dream to become a diplomat. I wondered where she wanted to go from here.

"I am happy with being a nurse. It is a good profession. I love languages and that will never change. I will go back to college once you have a permanent job."

I wanted her to get a college degree as soon as possible. I owed her that.

"If I had left you in Australia, we probably would have never married each other. You may have met someone else, and so would I. You and I could forever be in love because we would remember only the best of each other, but I chose you. Remember that." She told me the truth, the truth I had always known.

"We were kids then. We just followed our hearts." I reached for her hand. It was very soft.

"We still have each other." She squeezed back. "That's all I need."

The Mountain

My iPhone beeped. A Messenger text appeared from my brother Hòa, "Ba is seriously ill." He hardly ever messaged me so I knew it was time to go home if I wanted to see my father alive. Right away, I made arrangements for a ten-day trip to Vietnam to spend a few days with Ba at the farm in Tay Ninh. He had lived to be ninety-two, a lot longer than most men of his generation. Other than blood pressure medications that he used to take, he was totally drug-free. He had no pain in his limbs or his back and needed no assistance until the ripe age of ninety. He had lost his hearing but he still remembered everyone's name and asked me about them whenever I visited. Then he started to complain about pain the last two years as his body declined like a plane plunging straight down.

I knew that Ba didn't have much longer to live and I wished to spend the final days with him and maybe if my timing was good, I could see him through. I was totally prepared to be home just in time for his funeral.

Hòa and his family had been carrying the heavy burden of taking care of Ba in his old age. He did the same for Ma before because he was the only one who could. Other brothers in Saigon tried but in the big city, my father felt like a prisoner within the four walls of his room. Outside beyond the quiet alley, the noisy and smokey streets were packed with young people fighting for a living. At the farm, he could walk to the village church, the corner market and sit with a few old friends for a cup of coffee and a cigarette. The farm in Tay Ninh had become the nucleus for our clan. It is the place for the brothers to gather, for me to return. The nearby village cemetery has also become the place where I can come back to pay respects to my grandparents, Ma, and Phương.

Since Phương had died, my brother Hòa gradually transferred the farm management to his son Ti and daughter-in-law. Ti and Thao had diversified the farm to reduce their dependence on the chemicals that a mango farm needs. They had cut down rows of mango trees and planted coconut and mangosteen. Coconut needed no care while mangosteen yielded fruit through the summer and they fetched more money per kilo.

When I arrived at the farm this time, Ba was already half-dead. He was lying on a mattress in the room where my mother used to sleep. He could not sit up anymore and one leg was frozen in a folded position. His skeletal body was locked into a flat triangle that made changing and cleaning him difficult. He couldn't hear much, but he cracked a toothless smile when I said my name: "Con Xê đây, Ba ơi." His eyes were still clear—perhaps sharp vision is the best gene that he passed onto his sons. He pointed his bony finger at a mosquito as it flew around the room.

Hòa decided that it was best to have Dr. Dao come by every other day to give him an IV with proteins to sustain him and antibiotics to fight infections. Dr. Dao was a retired doctor who did home visits around the village. Hòa had known her for years since he was hospitalized after a traffic accident, and she healed him from a broken jaw. It was the best care Hòa could get for Ba, at the same costs of a hospital stay but Ba would be with family.

Dr. Dao also taught Ti how to clean the bedsores on Ba's back. The room smelled putrid with bacterial infections of his wounds. She taught Ti about bandages and disinfectants. She cut away the dead tissues as she talked, almost the way one orders dinner in a restaurant. Ba screamed every time she pulled out a piece of rotten flesh with the forceps. I tried not to look. Ti went outside and puked in his mask.

"With antibiotics in the IV, the wounds should heal in a few days." She stood up and went out to drink some tea with Hòa under the mango tree.

Every day, I spent a few hours with Ba but he mostly slept. When I visited five months back, he had been much more lucid and could talk. He was sitting against the wall with a walker in front of him, and I was listening to his babbling about random subjects. I could only understand half of what he said, but that was more than I had heard from him before—all the years put together. He hardly made any sense but occasionally I got some nuggets. I picked out some words as he mumbled and painted the air with his shaky arm: "…a mountain, Thai Son mountain.."

In the Chinese classics, a father is revered as a mountain, strong and solid, and a mother as the stream, clear and nourishing. Ba always thought of himself as the Thai Son mountain in Vietnam. In fact, his name, Tung, means vertical, straight up, unmovable.

He was born in Hue, central Vietnam, in 1928, the Year of the Dragon. He named his first born Hoành, meaning horizontal, like the sea. Together, *Tung Hoành* is the complete universe in perfect harmony, the best of Heaven and Earth.

I am number three in the lineup of his seven sons. My mother had wished so badly for a girl to keep her company and help her with housework, but the gods weren't kind. An uncle of mine has five girls and wants a boy. He asked Ba all the time how he managed to make seven sons. Ba always told his favorite sex joke: "Let me show you." He laughed out loud every time despite the embarrassment he caused my uncle. Seven sons in Vietnam means seven tigers while five girls are only five flowers.

When he turned eighteen, Ba was drafted into the colonial army just when the French were defeated in Dien Bien Phu and forced out of Southeast Asia. As the last grudging act, France arranged an agreement in Geneva to temporarily divide Vietnam in two halves pending a general election which never happened. The Americans had already got involved as the French were bowing out and wanted to stop the domino effect of communism. Vietnam became the battleground for the cold war between the U.S. and the Soviet Union.

When he was home, he wore his shorts and tank top, working on his homemade stereos and radios. He also got into collecting and fixing old wristwatches, which other officers sold to him for gambling money. Often, I'd see him crawling around the floor looking for the tiny gear or screws that fell down and rolled away. That's how he spent most of his time, looking for lost parts.

The first ten years of my life, my family was happy in Da Nang, a coastal city in central Vietnam. In 1965 when war was raging everywhere, Ba sought reassignment to a new post in Saigon for our safety. One day, Ba, Ma and seven kids packed a few bags and boarded a military C-130 with propellers, and flew south. I sat on a metal seat looking out the window at the green fields and coastline, scared of the plane's heaving through pockets of air turbulence.

In Saigon, we moved a lot, from one rental house to another and finally to a military base. Double-digit inflation ate away at Ba's income which was barely enough to buy rice for the seven growing boys. Ma's asthma got worse, along with the stress she felt about her sons' future, while Ba became more and more distant. He sought assignments to be away from home. He spent a few years in Can Tho, the largest town in the Mekong Delta. Ma suspected that Ba was unfaithful to her, and she yelled at Ba a lot which drove him further away. He didn't say much when he was home, not that we had ever talked before.

I wanted to be near him. I tried to get involved with his hobbies but I was no good at finding the lost parts. I would hold his hammer and screwdriver for him, hoping that would make the projects easier, but his repair projects usually ended up incomplete. He was no handyman. When I turned thirteen, I asked Ma to let me spend one summer with Ba in Can Tho, and she was glad I did. Can Tho was a gentle town on the south fork of the Mekong River that enriches the delta and feeds the country. I was in love with the green rice fields and Vọng Cổ music of southern people and the abundance of fish and tropical fruits. It was the longest time I spent with Ba alone, father and son, although I don't recall that we ever talked.

I was happy that summer in Can Tho. Every afternoon, I went fishing for little brown fish from the muddy bank using little ant eggs for bait. I took a water taxi with Ba one early morning to the floating market where large boats from all over the Delta came to trade their pumpkins, vegetables, rice bags, bananas, mangoes, pineapples, papayas, chickens and ducks. Food vendors navigated smaller boats between the larger ones selling steamed pork buns, sweet rice in banana leaves, and my favorite *chè*, sweet drinks of all kinds of beans and coconut milk.

Before I left for Australia, Ba took me out for Phở, and the two of us ate in silence, the way we always were together. When we were done, he pulled out a gold Seiko watch that he had been fixing. "This is automatic and will run forever if you take good care of it. Don't ever drop it in the water. Remember to have it oiled every ten years. One day it will be a classic." He wiped the lens with a fine cloth and tightened the strap for me. Then he gave me twenty dollars, his whole month of pay back then. Then we did not see each other for twenty years.

I was in Canberra when Giải Phóng happened in April 1975. I had written to tell him to go to the Australian embassy in Saigon and ask for help but I knew it was hopeless. The country was in chaos. He had a few American friends but they had already left. By the time I had contact with Ma through a contact in France several years later, Ma replied that he had been taken to a concentration camp up north where prisoners of war were supposed to die. Ma had been able to visit him once to bring him some clothes and dried foods.

Nobody expected him to survive the imprisonment but ten years later, Ma wrote: "Ba came home. He has a bad case of TB, lost all his teeth and so much weight. However, he has returned to the farm with us." I took out the bottle of Wild Turkey I had saved and drank a shot to celebrate—the whiskey tasted bitter but smooth.

When I first returned to Vietnam, he was skeletal but strong. He lived in a bamboo hut by himself a stone's throw from the family house on the farm. The first year of his return, Ma took great care of him, and they got along. Gradually old issues crept back. He asked what she had done with his stereos and record collection and got mad when she told him that she had sold all that to buy food for the kids. They argued every time they were within sight of each other. She would yell and he would sulk. So Hòa decided they whould be better off separate from each other and built him a separate house. Ba'd only come out for dinner then retreat to his cabin without saying a word. Hòa said that it took years to cure him of the TB. It took even longer for him to venture out beyond the barbed wire fence. It took ten years before he decided to turn his hut into a little classroom and teach English to the village kids. They paid him just enough for his coffee money.

One time I returned to the farm on one of my annual trips when Ma was alive. I always spent a few days at the farm to eat, sleep, and walk around the village. Ba came out a bit longer, and we sat down in a corner away from Ma's place. He grabbed my arm and laughed, the happiest I had heard him laugh in years:

"The Seiko! It is running, I told you."

Indeed, I took care of it. I dunked it once in the water at Virginia Beach and I quickly took it to a jeweler to clean before rust set in. He was in the mood to talk so I leaned back. He told me a bit about his early days. "The French rounded up young boys for their army. I was trained as an officer because I had a high school education and could read and write in French. After losing the final battles of Dien Bien Phu, they left after dividing Vietnam in two countries as a parting gift. I became an officer for the new South Vietnam whether I wanted to or not. Nobody ever asked."

In the South Vietnam military, he preferred a technical job and therefore was denied the promotions his cohorts received. Not only for that reason: he refused to be part of the corrupt system. "My fellow officers were selling copper telephone wires, gasoline, and US supplies in the black market. I know everyone who did it but I wouldn't rat on them. Even the generals were on the take so who could I trust? If I bent a little, maybe you and Ma could be better off, but I couldn't. I am just a silly stubborn man."

Every time I came back to visit, he seemed a bit stronger. He smiled and talked a bit more although he could barely hear anything. I was happy to sit under the mango tree and listen to any story he told. Often, it was about what he heard on the news with a twist of what he was indoctrinated in camp. "America is such a rich country. Life is so invaluable there, not like us here. One American life is worth hundreds of Vietnamese. Millions of us died during the war and they never mention that. You are lucky to live in America." He always made sure I got that.

"Why don't you come to live with us in America? If you don't like it, you can always return." I tempted him.

"What am I going to do there? I am already an old man. What about Ma and your brothers here? Ma doesn't want to go anywhere and your brothers already have wives and kids."

Then after my mother died in 2001, Ba applied for the last round of orderly departure for ex-officers and was granted immigrant status to the U.S. He came to live the remaining years with his three sons in the United States. It would be an adventure for him. He would see the Statue of Liberty, eat hamburgers and French fries, drive in nice cars, watch his granddaughters grow and be part of their lives.

Staggering off the big airplane, Ba shuffled slowly down the long jetway at San Francisco Airport, carrying only a white plastic bag with a big red cross on its side. Inside the bag were a shirt and a pair of trousers, a toothbrush and a disposable razor. His scuffed leather shoes had been bleached under the tropical sun and softened by rain. He looked lost in the cathedral-ceilinged airport filled with crowded bars, restaurants, and luxurious gift shops.

His English was sufficient to lead him to the arrival area where he hoped to find his sons. After embracing his sons and daughters-in-law, he reached out his hand to touch the girls' hair—they recoiled and hid behind their parents' legs, eyes round. The twenty-hour flight had exhausted him. He coughed a little from the nagging pain in his lungs, shocked by the blast of cold air outside the airport. My oldest brother Hoành took him home in a brand-new Honda Accord and showed him the house in a quiet neighborhood of San Jose. His wife made the guest room tidy and comfortable for him. He skipped the first meal and slept for twenty-four hours straight.

He stayed with each of his sons for two or three months at a time and we took him out every weekend to show him America. The honeymoon with us was glorious. Hoành took him to Las Vegas, Yosemite, Tahoe, Napa Valley, Orange County, and I did many other states in the East. He saw in a year what many Americans don't see in a lifetime. Hoành had picnics and BBQs for him every sunny summer weekend in his San Jose backyard. The grilled lemongrass chicken and hot dog smoke rose, cold beer filled large coolers, well-to-do Vietnamese mingled to talk business and vacations, and many a Lexus and Mercedes parked in the street.

Once, Hoành took him to San Francisco for a day trip to see the Pacific Ocean, Chinatown, Fisherman's Wharf, and the Golden Gate Bridge. From Fort Baker, he admired the two giant pillars and the red cables suspending the one-mile span half hidden in the thick fog.

He had seen fog like this before, he told me. The Xiang Xi Pang mountains separating North Vietnam and China rise straight up and have kept Vietnam from being swallowed by its Chinese neighbors to the North. His labor camp rested just below the clouds, and from there, he could see the green rice terraces below and a bamboo forest separating him and his fellow POWs from their previous lives. Their daily tasks were to climb the steep slope looking for large trees to cut and skid them downhill to be sawn and sold. Human termites: that's what they were.

The only human contact they had besides their keepers were the Muong tribal villagers. in the hills. The concentration camp for officers was carved out of the forest near where the tribes grew their crops and kept their goats. The tribes were the last of the natives who were on the losing end of a struggle for independence. One day, the low-land people would move up to take their land and drive them further up into the mountain clouds. He could feel compassion in their eyes, and they glanced askance at the prisoners walking by on a daily labor march. Occasionally, he would find a bit of rice packed in banana leaf on a bamboo fence; sometimes, boiled sweet potato or cassava.

Each day, the young guard with an AK-47 hanging by his side gave them a long standard lecture in a pure northern country accent before sending them to the field to work: "Here, there are no officers, no privates, no ranks. You are all prisoners! You have been traitors and enemies of the people. You have destroyed our country by working for the false regime and the American invaders. They are murderers and rapists. You deserve to die for your crimes. However, the leniency of Uncle Ho and the party spares your life. You are lucky to have the chance to redeem yourselves and serve the new regime…"

He and his fellow officers were forced to write their confessions every night. Some wrote what they thought was true, but the keepers tore it up and told them to begin again. Finally, they got smart and wrote exactly what they heard daily. That did the trick: all confessions looked the same.

When he talked about those years, he still reminisced about the beauty of the northern mountains as if he'd been on vacation. His daily route took him across cold clear streams that held fish. Hornbills and pheasants passed overhead. Butterflies swarmed every clearing and fed on dung. Tigers had been sighted in the foggy jungle above the camp, so they always made a lot of noise where they worked. Large trees at these high elevations had been spared during the war. No roads reached these forests back then. He and his fellows were the first humans to reach them and then cut them down with axes and handsaws. He wondered how long this place would last before being denuded and converted to coffee and tea plantations.

Despite all our efforts to care for him, we all had to work and the children went to school. Weekends in America were always exciting, but he dreaded the weekdays, especially winter days that reminded him of Xiang Xi Pang. In his bones, he still felt the dampness of the jungle camp that sapped his body of whatever it had left. At night in the mountain fog, he rolled himself like a shrimp on the hard bamboo cot. The torn military blanket barely covered his skinny body. The prisoners had stopped complaining about hunger and the cold. Those who complained had died already within a month of their arrival. In fact, those with less disciplined appetites were the first to go because they ate everything they could find. Dysentery was the most effective killer.

The winter in Silicon Valley hit him with a different coldness: A dry cold wind on sunny days blisters the skin and burns it at the same time. Every weekday morning, after his son and daughter-in-law left for work and the children went to school, the old man was all alone in the house. He put on layers of thermal underwear, a flannel shirt, a thick sweater, and a wool coat, plus a hat and gloves, and went for a daily walk. His disciplined lifestyle kept him alive. He walked a few miles around the neighborhood and looked at the wood-framed houses with gray composite and fake tile roofs. A bedroom community, all the cars had disappeared for the day, and the dogs didn't bark. In America, dogs don't bark or bite, and he even missed the noisy pack dogs at the farm.

All day, he walked and thought about his wife, his sons, their children, and where he would call home. He had thought about them every day in Xiang Xi Pang with little hope of ever seeing them again. Prisoners were dying from infections, diseases, accidents, and starvation. The guards didn't have to beat them—lack of food and medical supplies plus hard labor took them out one by one. However, in San Jose, he missed the companionship. At least in the "death camp," talking to fellow officers kept him sane. They swapped stories about their families, their earlier heroic exploits, and their misspent youth, and passed around occasional morsels of food and sips of homebrew.

One weekend, my two brothers and I huddled together to discuss how to give Ba a social life. "He is home all the time, no one to talk to. He won't do anything and watches Vietnamese music videos all day long." Hoành lamented. "I think we should put him near Little Saigon within walking distance of the Vietnamese markets and the new immigrants. Maybe that's more like home."

"What does Ba think?" Ho looked at his feet.

"How did he do last time he was staying with you?" Hoành countered. "We all tried. Nothing worked." Brother Hoành threw his beer bottle at the wall "Stop!" That was the end of that.

We found him a room to share with a Vietnamese family in

a neighborhood near Little Saigon. He could walk to the market place to buy food, hang out with fellow refugees his age, and socialize in Vietnamese.

Every now and then, I took a day off and picked him up for lunch. In the windowless room in the shared house, he'd made himself a cocoon with his cot surrounded by clutter of junk. During his daily walks, he collected beer bottle caps of different kinds. With his weekly visits to the flea market, he amassed a fortune of collectibles: old transistor radios, various portable television sets, cooking utensils, electronic clocks, a few tools that he might one day need, all for a dollar each. In Vietnam, these were worth plenty. That's all he could afford now and they kept him company and filled the emptiness in his room.

One day at the Phở restaurant, he told me that he had recently gone in for a checkup on his prostate cancer. The doctor said: "You are in excellent health, for your age. We can treat you, and you may live ten years. We can leave it alone and you may live ten years. What do you want to do?" It was a no-brainer. That's when he made a decision to get a one-way ticket and go back to the farm.

We sat under the big mango tree listening to the cicadas sing in the dark. "Anh Xê, have some tea," Hòa poured me a cup and lit me a cigarette.

"Ba wants you to have this." Hòa handed me a student notebook. "He said to give it to you after he dies. Since this is the last time you see him alive, here it is."

I found a quiet corner that evening and opened his book. His penmanship was excellent, although it trailed severely near the end.

To Con Xê:

You are the most precious gift my wife gave me. They say she bred like a hen: two babies every three years, plump happy ones, full of life. You came into a world of war and poverty without a care, laughing and eating everything we gave you.

When you were young, I used to take the family out for treats after Sunday church. I would have a cup of drip coffee; your mother sipped a glass of orange juice, and we watched you savor hot sweet buns with red beans inside served with small scoops of vanilla ice cream.

You ate a lot. My salary as a military officer was barely enough to buy thirty kilos of rice a month. Each day your mother cooked a huge rice pot and you ate it all. You even fought for the crispy burned rice stuck to the bottom of the pot. I wondered how I could feed seven growing boys. I am grateful to God that after all these years, you are still all alive. It is a miracle that you managed to survive. I did too.

We named you for peace and harmony, and you were always the quiet and undemanding one. You won a scholarship and then came home one day to tell us that you were going to college overseas, all expenses paid. You did all that on your own. I couldn't have paid for any of it—far too much money for me to imagine, but you left on a large plane with fifty best and brightest kids in the country to a place far away.

Do you remember that before you left, I took you out for Phở one morning and we sat for one hour without saying a word? Your mother and I saw you off at Tân Sơn Nhất airport and we thought that we would never see you again. I hope the Seiko watch is still ticking.

I often wonder how to talk to you? What can I talk about? All my life, I have never really talked to anyone. I didn't talk to my father who died young. My mother never talked to me; she worked long hours every day. I fed my brothers and sisters and watched them get sick and die but I didn't know what to say. I don't remember talking to your mother either. I loved her and she was crazy about me.

I am not sure if I could have done anything for your Ma. Had she lived in America, they might have had treatments to help her. She had a very tough life taking care of seven kids. She worried day to day about you and I was absent most of the time. Even in the last few years when the farm was doing well, she woke up every day sad and angry and threw things at me. The wires in her mind had shorted. She died mad.

San Jose is not the America I imagined as in a Hollywood movie. In San Jose, I see people like you, immigrants from Vietnam, China, and India, working for computer companies. The rest are poor Mexican construction workers, mowing and blowing, and selling tacos from trucks. White people don't live here in this part of the valley. The Grand Century Mall food court sells Phở, pancakes, salted lemonade, sugar cane juice, and all kinds of che`. It would be a great place to take my grandchildren out, but they say these malls are so ethnic. They prefer the Gap and Macy's.

I enjoyed your rare visits. You worked and traveled a lot, and you lived sixty miles away. Every once in a while, you called me up: "Let's go to lunch." You asked me often: "Ba, why don't you write down for me your story—the story of your life? I want to know, and I don't know anything about you. Tell me how much you made when you were a military officer? How was prison camp?

Did they torture you?" You asked too many questions that I don't want to answer. I usually said: "Nobody appreciates my story. It's all sad and full of bad news. I don't write anything down anymore. I will get punished for that." You seemed grateful for every bit of time you had with me, then you dropped me off at the house and drove back to work.

My name is Tung for vertical, standing tall, and uncompromising. It didn't help me make money, while all my friends did. I have lived long enough. I have seen many wars. I served a defeated regime, survived ten years in a jungle camp, and yet I am still breathing.

I watched my wife die, and my sons starve. Some left for America and the rest labored on a desolate farm.

I am writing to you to say goodbye. Here at the farm, I live among poor people, but I will die where I was born. I will be near your mother's grave, and I will visit her every Sunday to tell her I am sorry. I will be with your other brothers, who still have time for me. I will take my grandchildren to the markets and buy them ice cream and hot sweet buns, and they will hold my hands on my sunset walks, and together, we will watch the dragonflies hover above the village canal.

That was also the last night before I had to leave to go back to America. Before the car came to pick me up around noon the next day, Thao cooked him a bowl of rice gruel and let me feed him, spoon by spoonful. Ba lay on a mattress surrounded by boxes of Ensure and diapers. We changed him one more time. Even with antibiotics, his bed sores were atrocious. I held him when Ti cleaned his wounds. "See! I can see his bones." His shaved head felt like wet sandpaper.

"Please! Stop! Oh, the pain!" he screamed.

"Shhh, Shhhh," I whispered in his ear.

Ba oi!, Dad! Please die. Oh God! Let him die.

Another Tết

To Americans, Tết is bad news. The Tết Offensive was the beginning of the end of the American involvement in Southeast Asia. Body bags came home, sometimes hundreds a day. The loss was more than this country could bear and broke the morale of even the richest and most powerful country on earth.

In Vietnam, Tết simply means a few days of the lunar new year when the Vietnamese farmers stop working in the field after the harvests, and factory workers have a few days off. Families gather to celebrate life, remember the dead, and pray to the gods for happiness and health and a good year without famine, floods, fire, and the ever-present war. Tết is a joyous time. For a few days, everyone comes home. No matter where they toil, they return to visit their parents, the village or farm, and where their ancestors are buried.

For me, the place to return has been the mango farm in Tay Ninh, where my parents had lived with brother Hòa and his family since Giải Phóng in 1975. I had been back for Tết a few times after twenty years in exile. In America, Thanksgiving and Christmas holidays are similar to Tết. Family members get together, give each other gifts, and enjoy a feast. These holidays came to mean little to me since I lived many years in the Midwest and the East Coast, far from my brothers and my in-laws in California and Ba Ma in Vietnam. I'd saved up money and time to go home to Vietnam for Tết, but sometimes I just couldn't.

When I found Ma again in 1994 during my first trip back, I swore I would come to see her every Tết, a promise I couldn't keep. I still regret that I didn't come back more often than the seven times I did before she died. After our first reunion at Tân Sơn Nhất airport, I stepped back into the world of my boyhood. I relived the street noise, the bad air, and the griminess of heat and humidity. Every Celtis tree and noodle stand along the roads brought a rush of memories. At my brother Bê's tiny place in an alley, Ma cooked a meal to treat my American friends and me the same way she had treated my high school friends before I left Saigon. She had on her best clothes: a brown tunic with little white dots and black silk pantaloons. They hung loosely on her as if she were a coat hanger. Her long hair was still thick but more silver than black and tied back in a bun. Her bony hands shook constantly, but she stood to serve my friends the chicken curry with cut-up baguettes. Harold nudged me, "She is so proud of you." She put her hands together in prayer and bowed to my friends. She told me to thank them for bringing me home. After a few days, I went to Tram Chim Park with my friends for a week and came back to Saigon to stay with her for a while.

"How is Ba?" I wondered why he didn't come to Saigon with her.

"He is sick, so he stays at the farm," she said flatly. I asked what ailed him, and she just replied that he couldn't travel.

The next day, Bê took Ma and me back to the farm in Tay Ninh by bus. Back then, there were no cars to hire, and the bus took four hours to go one hundred kilometers due to bad roads. The farm was a patch of dry land with a few cashew trees and a single mango tree that Ma had planted when they first got there. It grew from a seed the size of a baby's hand and was now the biggest tree that provided shade to the family bamboo and thatched house. Around the house were rows of potatoes, cassava, and okra. Hòa and Phương had just started to grow mango trees. "Look! Anh Xê, we should have fruit in two years!" Phương beamed as she soaked the cashew nuts in a bucket to ensure they weighed more. "We have chickens. They can fly, these chickens. We can catch them at night in the trees." She laughed like a chime.

Ba was in his hut when I found him. His hairline had receded to the back of his head and his goatee was all white. He wore only a pair of faded red, loose-fitting shorts that went down to his knees. From the waist up, I could see every rib and a hollow stomach, but his voice was strong.

"Ba mạnh khoẻ không?" I asked about his health.

"You sound like a Việt Kiều," he laughed, his ill-fitting dentures clacking. "Like someone reading a line on TV." I wasn't speaking fluently after twenty years of little practice. It took me a minute to get used to the darkness inside the hut. It was minimalist with a bamboo bed, a few pots and pans, a calendar on the wall with pictures of flowers and smiling kids, and a transistor radio.

"I am fine. Just a little coughing in the night. Otherwise, I am going to live another thirty years." He got up and led me outside; we sat on his veranda looking at the forsythia and jasmine plants around his hut. As before, we found little to say. I stole a few pictures of him with my camera while he looked at the sky with a blank expression as in deep meditation.

"Dinner time!" Hòa came over to the hut to get me. I got up to go back to the farm house but Ba remained at his hut. "Ba eats alone. We bring him food here," Hòa grimaced.

Under the mango tree, I ate dinner with Ma and Hòa's family. It was a simple meal with boiled potato leaves dipped in fish sauce with crushed hard-boiled eggs, a thin pumpkin soup and salted fish. With steaming rice, the light food was delicious.

After dinner, Hòa and I shared tea and cigarettes in the flickering kerosene lamp light. "It's like a cold war," he explained, "If Ma is here, Ba is not. If Ba is here, Ma is not. They are the sun and the moon. They can't share the same sky."

"It was good for a while," Hòa tapped his ash on the dirt floor. "When Ba first came home, she took good care of him. She saved him from sure death when he coughed up blood. She stayed with him at the hospital and fed him. When he was better, they fought again. Over nothing. I make decisions about the farm, not about their problems. They should relax and enjoy the last few years of their lives, but still, there is always something. That's why I had to separate them."

I witnessed the détente between Ba and Ma for three full days. Perhaps, the ten years at the concentration camp had done him in. Maybe the trauma of Giải Phóng had stressed her out. Maybe time would heal. I bid goodbye to Ba and returned with Ma to Saigon to meet up with my friends before we headed back to America.

Ma was the center of her sons' lives, while Ba was like a satellite circling around in orbit. Ever since the family moved from Da Nang to Saigon when I turned ten, he was at home less and less. He would come home for a week every few months and then leave again to live in a different town. Unlike her sister, who complained about Uncle Đúng being at sea and leaving her alone to take care of the kids, Ma never complained about Ba's absence. She was ill and frail most of the time, and I took over some of the chores, like going to the market and cooking meals. "I wish we had a *người làm* (live-in help), but I can't afford that anymore," she sighed. "We had always had someone before when we lived in Da Nang."

Ma had always treated *người làm* like a family member when we had one in Da Nang. They were usually farm girls or women who came to the city to work for families like ours. Back then, before the war intensified and inflation made Ba's salary worthless, a military officer or an office worker made enough to pay the rent, feed the kids, and hire one *người làm*. She cooked, cleaned, took care of the kids, and lived in the house in exchange for meals, some spending money, and a trip home for Tết every year. The last *người làm* we had was Chị Bẩy. She was ten years older than Hoành and tougher than buffalo meat. She was a stout woman who was never sick and did the chores with a smile. Her cooking was not great, so Ma took time to teach her to make fish sauce dip the way Ba liked it. She was like an older sister to me, but we left her in Da Nang when the family moved to Saigon in 1965.

In Saigon, I learned to shop and cook rice since Ma developed chronic asthma. In Vietnamese, *nấu cơm* (cooking rice) literally means making the whole meal, and *ăn cơm* (eating rice) means having a meal together. *Cơm* was the central part of daily family life, at least the life I knew. Being the oldest of the brothers now, I helped Ma with *nấu cơm*. Ma had taught me the routines of food shopping:

"You have to bargain! Don't be shy. If they say ten piasters, you say five. If they say eight, you walk away. They will call you back, and then you have a fair deal."

"When the bananas and papayas start to have black dots on their skin, they are really soft and sweet for a very short time in this heat. If not sold fast, they will be thrown away to the pigs. You can get the best price for them. Your hungry brothers, and you will finish them in a day anyway." She stroked my hair, tears in her eyes.

I learned quickly and was deft with chopping vegetables, slicing meat, and even killing a chicken now and then. I hated slaughtering chickens every Tết. Only on such occasions, the family could afford to put a couple of chickens to death to prepare a feast for the extended family. I learned how to hold the chicken wings down with one knee and put a sharp knife to its neck. The blood would drain into a bowl until the chicken stopped struggling and went limp in my hands.

At night, I tossed and turned, listening to Ma's wheezing and the clearing of her throat. Some nights, she would sit up in her bed sweating and breathing heavily. I tried to cool her off with a paper fan and rub eucalyptus oil on her back; somehow, that helped. I also became known at the local pharmacy—the women there had a constant supply of antihistamine pills ready for me to pick up.

"We know this is what your mother needs. If she needs more pills to fortify her heart, we have many kinds." They always offered to sell more drugs.

Ma came from a wealthy family. Ông Ngoại (my grandfather) was a merchant from Canton who married a Vietnamese woman and established a machine shop in the middle of Da Nang, the largest coastal city in central Vietnam. Ma had a high school education, and back then, that was good enough for office work. She got a job with a decent salary working for a French company in

Da Nang. Other than *người làm*, Vietnamese women didn't work outside the home. Ma was ahead of her time perhaps because she was half-Chinese and wasn't bound by Vietnamese traditions, which men made up to keep women inside their homes. The French had already changed Vietnamese society by hiring female secretaries, and Ma was among the first. She ignored the ridicule and name-calling by the other women in town. *Con Xẩm*, they called her, the Chinese Girl, and worse yet, "French whore." Ma didn't care about what others said of her being half-Chinese, and of course, Ông Ngoại was open-minded and taught her to be independent. She spoke good French and learned to drive a car with a stick shift.

Once, she drove a British Hillman across the Hai Van pass between Da Nang and Hue, maybe a first for Vietnamese women. She had three suitors in her office, and they invited her to join their acting class. They were putting on a play and offered her a part in it. That's when she met Ba, who was also learning to act. Ba was poor, but he was handsome, so she liked him best. One day, the police came and took the three men away to prison. She learned later that they were with the subversive Viet Minh resistance and were infiltrating the French organization. She married Ba, got pregnant with Hoành, and quit the company to be a housewife just before Ba was drafted into the army.

In Da Nang, she was a happy homemaker. With the dowry Ông Ngoại gave her, she bought a small house where we grew up. She kept hoping for a baby girl, but one boy came after another, all seven of us. After number seven, she gave up. Ma was a mother hen who kept us under her wings all the time, as long as she could. In Saigon, she was sick a lot, Ba was gone most of the time, and the war came closer to home. She couldn't protect us anymore and gave up trying. "All I can do is give you roots to grow. The rest is up to God." She often told me, "Nothing is more important than the heart. A man must have a clean and generous heart. Remember that, Con Xê."

One year I came home for Tết when Hòa and Phương were already doing well with the Mango farm. The farmhouse had been rebuilt with bricks and cinder blocks and the floor was paved with smooth ceramic tiles. The village finally had electricity, so we didn't need the kerosene lamps. The mango trees were heavy with fruit, and trucks came in every day to ship tons of mangoes to Saigon.

From the back of the house, the burning of fish sauce and wood smoke wafted across the yard. Hòa and his wife Phương finished the day's work in the field. They came home with two catfish still wiggling on a string. The fish were caught when the villagers drained a pond to sell their tilapias, snakeheads, and eels at the Tết market.

The catfish turned crispy in the bubbly oil. As soon as their skin cracked, Phương scooped them out onto a large plate and put a wire mesh lid over them to keep the flies out. Later, she served them with fresh herbs, rice vermicelli, pickled radish, and carrot, all wrapped together in moist rice paper.

The yellow Mai flowers bloomed along the dirt driveway leading to the house. Growers timed their flowering perfectly by stripping off the leaves to force the trees into dormancy. Hòa had learned to do this well—he had the reputation as the most successful farmer in the village.

I found Ma in the house with the electric fan running. "Mother, how is your asthma?"

She handed me a small jar of eucalyptus oil, and I knew exactly what to do. I rubbed the oil on her skinny back and scraped it gently with a copper coin until her skin turned scarlet. In time, the bruised areas would become black and blue, and she would feel better because the *bad wind* would be pushed out with the *bad blood*.

After the back rub, her breathing improved. I made her a lemonade with the limes from the garden. As we sat together near the window to get some air, Ma told me she wanted to give me something. She emptied the contents of a rusty tin box onto the kitchen table next to the window. Her hands caressed photographs of her boys and one of her with her husband on their honeymoon trip to Dalat. Her eyes blurred a little with wetness. She couldn't see well anymore, distant or close-up.

"I want you to have these photographs and letters. These are the only things I have for you."

She showed me a letter in which I wrote to say I would not make it home for Tết. In the U.S., there is no time off from work to celebrate Tết.

A photo of my brothers and me made her smile. It was taken when we were kids, and the family was still together. We were wearing the aloha shirts with hibiscus flowers she made for us when she still could thread a needle. Our chubby legs lined up like French baguettes, we straddled a bench and looked sideways with silly grins, so carefree. We were her pride and joy—her whole world. Now three of us lived overseas, and for many years she had not seen us.

She dug out a postcard I wrote to her, postmarked in Singapore right after I left Saigon to go to college in Australia:

"Dear Ba Ma, I am in transit here. They put me up in a great big hotel in the middle of the airport, as big as a city. I am well. Please don't worry about me because I can take care of myself now. I will write every week. Your son, always."

I did keep that promise. I wrote to her every week, and she tucked the letters under her pillow until they got to be too many, then she kept them in a tin box next to her bed.

I wrote about taking English classes and getting ready for university. I missed her cooking and learned to eat new foods like eggs and bacon, lamb chops, and spaghetti in red meat sauce. I sent a few color photos I took in front of big buildings, one with falling brown leaves and another with snow and frozen trees.

She handed me the box and told me to keep it. I didn't want to, but she said, "Now that I have found you again, I don't need all this. I don't have long to live, so you should have it to remember me."

It is priceless.

"Thank you for the money you sent," she reminded me of the savings I used to send home when twenty dollars could feed the family for two months. "Thank you for saving Hoành and Ho. Nobody did more for the family than you."

"I wish I could do more." I meant what I said, but I couldn't do much more during those early years after Giải Phóng. I had never told her about my struggles to survive as a foreign student and an immigrant. How could I? My life was so different from the life she knew. The two worlds had no overlap. Most Vietnamese imagined life in America as heaven on earth, and every Việt Kiều drove new cars and lived in big houses.

"I know you did everything you could. I have one more favor to ask: I hope to see this before I die." Her clouded eyes watered. "Can you take Ba with you?" she pleaded. I had asked Ba before, and he didn't answer.

"What about you, Ma? Will you go?"

"No, I am too old and tired. I don't have long to live, and I will only be a burden to you."

I held her. She felt like bones held together in a sack and smelled like eucalyptus oil. She was happy for a day, but that didn't last long. The following days, she returned to all the bad things Ba had done.

"Your father has been in trouble again with the neighbors. He had an argument with Mr. Thanh over the fence and the next day there was a fire across the street. Nobody knew the source, but Ba did it. I am sure he did it."

I knew Ba could be mischievous but had he gone mad?

"Where is Ba now?" I hadn't seen him since I arrived.

"I don't know. Every time he got the money that you sent him from America, he disappeared for weeks. He wanted to rent a place in Tay Ninh city. He said the farm got boring."

"Why are you still married to him? You are no good for each other." I said it more like a statement than a question.

"I married into a Catholic family, and divorce is out of the question. I stayed with Ba for you, all of you. Society frowns upon a broken family, so I had to keep up the appearance. Ba only cares about his own needs. He is the oldest son, but he doesn't even take care of his own siblings. He never took care of you. It was always my responsibility."

"Did you get an earful?" Hòa cracked a crooked smile later under the mango tree. "I hear this all the time. Everyday. It is like a tape that is replayed over and over. She tells everyone the same story now. Everybody has heard this tape. I know it by heart."

Indeed, Ma no longer kept her complaints within the family. She couldn't help herself anymore. She could go on all day with the same monologue as long as she had an audience.

One day, Hoành came back from California to visit, and Ma visited him at his in-laws' house in Saigon. After a few minutes of questions and answers with the other elders about each other's health issues, Ma launched into her usual laments about Ba in front of everyone, to the parents of my brother's wife.

"Stop, Ma. Please," Hoành pleaded. "This is embarrassing."

Ma was unstoppable.

"STOP! ENOUGH!" Hoành stormed out of the room. He was breathing hard. His hands shook as he lit a cigarette.

After that incident, she stopped talking to Hoành. She refused to take any money that he sent her. She called him an ingrate, the harshest verdict against an ungrateful and uncaring son.

The last time I saw Ma was Tết of the year 2000. She was as gloomy as a thunderstorm. She had lost all interest in talking or even lamenting. I wanted so much for her to hold me and tell me she loved me, but her eyes glazed over. I asked her to tell me her story, anything. I was willing to listen. Finally, the night before I left to go back, she summoned all her strength as we sat under the mango tree.

"My dear son. I am sorry to have to tell you the truth. I wanted to round up all seven of you to clear my heart before I die, but that's not going to happen. So I am telling you, Con Xê. Please do not hate Ba, but I must speak. I don't hate Ba, but I despise him."

The dam broke.

"We were very happy in Da Nang. I was pregnant with the last boy, but there were complications, and I had to stay in the hospital for two months. I had a cesarean section to save number seven, and it took three more weeks to heal. When I got home, Ba said that Chị Bảy was a bad *người làm*. He said she had been stealing food money and didn't feed you enough. He told me that I must let her go. So I called her in and talked to her. She cried and didn't say anything. She didn't answer my questions and only said she wanted to go back to the farm, so I gave her some money, and she went away. I thought that was the end of that."

"A few months later, I was in the marketplace, and other women were gossiping. As I walked by, they stopped talking. I came to my father's house, and your Ông Ngoại scolded me, 'Why did you do that? How could you be so cruel? How could you send a pregnant woman away? You didn't do anything wrong, but it's your responsibility. You must take responsibility.' I was so shocked. I just didn't know."

"From then on, I couldn't love Ba again. I tried to put it behind me, but nothing worked. I had lost total respect for him, and nothing could repair that. We moved from Da Nang to Saigon to start over, to get away from the shame. I can live with his betrayal of me, but I can't forgive his cruelty to Chị Bảy and the unborn baby."

Her sorrows crushed me. In front of me was a woman who had been carrying two heavy baskets hanging at the ends of a stout bamboo stick. Every day, she had walked barefoot down the unpaved road toward the market place with the load bouncing with her steps. A straw hat protected her from the scorching sun. In one basket, she kept her seven sons. In the other, all her worries about keeping them alive through the war and famine. The old bamboo stick rested in the hollow between her neck and shoulder with sharp jolts of pain and a secret she hid to keep the family together. How could Ma bear it for this long? How can anyone bear it at all without going mad? I held her, and we both cried. I cried for her. I cried for my broken family. I cried for Chị Bảy and the baby.

She died the next year, I am sure of a broken heart. I came home for the funeral a few days late. Ba was at the farm. I saw him sit under the mango tree for hours, his hand caressing a rosary.

"You were too young to know," Hoành told me when we sat in his backyard having a beer. "Every family has a shameful secret. Somewhere in Da Nang, we have a half-brother or maybe a sister. We will never know, but with Ba's history, I'd bet on another boy."

Back Casts

The yellow fly line unfurled about seventy feet in front of me, and the tiny piece of red yarn dropped gently inside a round target on the quiet water of the pond—a well-executed cast with a 5-weight floating line. I had been at this game for about two years, faithfully every Sunday morning at 8 am sharp with a cup of coffee for me and one for John, my coach. "Good throw!" he yelled from across the pond.

The Oakland Casting Club nests in a quiet neighborhood near Highway 13, high above Berkeley. Tall redwood trees protect casters from gusty winds and give us a feel of the woods even though it is only fifteen minutes from downtown San Francisco. Regular members are mostly retired men, have money, love to show off their gear, and talk about big fish in exotic locations. Some are world-class bullshit artists. Some of them don't even fish; they are in it just for the Zen of the casts.

John is only a couple of years older than I am, which makes him a baby boomer, an age group that can't escape unemployment. The 2008 mortgage crisis had recently put skilled construction workers like him out of work. He discreetly inserted a wad of chewing tobacco into his lower lip, and his Hulk Hogan mustache moved a little to accommodate it. His eyes smiled as he received the cup of Peet's coffee, regular, no sugar, no milk. "Why ruin a perfectly good coffee?" he said. His muscular body moved slowly with stiff ankles, achy knees, and a bad back. A lifetime of hard labor.

"It is all about the loop; let the loop teach you," he spat at the ivy-covered fence. "There is only so much energy you can put into throwing that line. You must make all of it count." Minimum effort for maximum impact—the idea of *Chi*.

My friends often ask me why I am obsessed with fly fishing: "Why do you go through all that trouble when a few worms on a treble hook will catch any fish? Why not sit on a cooler full of cold Budweiser and let the fish come to you?" I usually give a flippant answer, "It's not about the fish." My Vietnamese compatriots don't see the point; they fish to fill freezers. I usually don't bother to give a full explanation because it would take too long to disclose my whole life journey, with many rivers and fish to tell of along the way.

My grandfather introduced me to fishing when I was a little boy growing up in Da Nang. Both Ma's parents had thick, beautiful black hair and Ông Ngoại paid my brothers and me one piaster for every white hair we pulled for him. A piaster was not much; a popsicle cost one hundred of them. I could do it in an hour with my little fingers, but I didn't understand why this deal continued way into his old age when his hair grew thinner and was more salt than pepper. Later in life, I finally understood: he enjoyed having us visit and hang around him. It was his way of fishing, and we were his fish.

I loved to go with him to the bank of the Da Nang River and watch him fish with a long bamboo pole arching over the slow-flowing water. Occasionally we came home with a red perch the size of a dinner plate, and he fried it Chinese style. To the crispy golden fish, he added hot peanut oil, soy sauce, julienne spring onions, and ginger on top. Of course, every fisherman has the one that got away. He often talked about a fish that took his worm, yanked him into the river, and broke the line. It must have been a huge river monster catfish!

The first ten years of my childhood in Da Nang were the happiest before I became aware of the killing, the bombs, and the hunger when we ran out of rice. In Saigon, my brother Bê and I looked for places to fish, but there were few. When desperate, we even tried the brown water of the log pond, and the sawmill workers laughed at us. The creek near our house was choked with garbage and stank of raw sewage. Only mosquito larvae lived there. Bê often got me in trouble poaching private ponds. One time, we caught a few small carp the size of three fingers when a neighbor wasn't home. They were so pretty with gold and silver scales we didn't want to kill them. We kept them alive in a bucket, but they turned belly up within an hour. When I turned thirteen, Ba took me to Can Tho for the summer, and I spent every afternoon on the Mekong river bank with a can of ant eggs. I caught many plump brown sculpins the size of bread sticks. They were delicious, braised in fish sauce and caramel. It was not that I needed to fish for food. There was something about waiting for a bite, watching the float dip down, and feeling the vibrations beneath the surface that signaled life, another type of life that I didn't know but was so mysterious and inviting.

I was fascinated with life beneath the water's surface, something I didn't see, but I longed for a connection. Sometimes, that life broke through the surface like the flying fish darting ahead of the bow of the *Trường Hải* when uncle Đúng took me on a trip along the coast of Vietnam in 1972, the year before I left Saigon. The winged fish were telling me that I would soon leave the world I knew to embark on a journey full of mystery to discover on my own.

Fishing was not on the agenda for many years when I became a foreign student in Australia and later a reluctant immigrant in America. In graduate school, I slipped out a few nights to soak pieces of squid off the Berkeley pier and caught flounders in San Francisco Bay. I heard about mercury in the bay, but I figured a little bit wouldn't kill me. However, there was nothing spectacular to report for the first ten years in America. It was mostly work, school, and sending money home to help Ba, Ma, and my brothers.

The best thing that happened to me during that time was having two brothers in my life. They escaped Vietnam with the boat people, and I bailed them out of the refugee camp in Malaysia and brought them to San Jose. Upon becoming a U.S. citizen and finishing the Ph.D. program at Berkeley, I applied for many teaching jobs at universities across the country and was rejected by all. I had a few bites for post-doc positions, but I was looking for stability, not more temporary gigs for subsistence. At last, I landed an offer from the Forest Service Research as a scientist at the prestigious Forest Products Laboratory (FPL) in Madison, WI. The hardest work to gain a footing in America was now complete, and I could look forward to new adventures.

July 4, 1986, Diep and I drove from Berkeley to Madison in our blue Renault Alliance. We stopped by Lake Tahoe, Yellowstone National Park, the Corn Palace, and the badlands of South Dakota; we traversed the magnificent Rockies and the Great Plains. Diep was not as excited as I was since she had a tough time leaving her parents behind again, but this time, we swore to return in a few years. After all, we were not in Australia anymore.

We would not need a passport and visa to get back to California. The air was hot and stagnant as we drove into town. It took no more than fifteen minutes to get from the west to the east end, and then we were in the middle of green corn fields. I turned the car around to head in the other direction, and sure enough, there was more corn on the other side. "That's it?" I thought. Diep phoned her parents as soon as we stopped at a supermarket. She had been crying the whole road trip, and now she burst into tears.

I drove by the FPL twice as I passed back and forth on Campus Drive. It was an old building, art deco as they call it, built-in 1910 at the edge of the University of Wisconsin campus, near many agricultural schools and a big cow barn. Diep cried even more when we checked in at the Motel Royal at the east end of town. It was cheap, and I could only afford the cheapest for two weeks while we looked for a rental apartment. The sirens went off as we checked in. "What's that?" I asked the front desk. "Tornado warning! Let's get to the shelter." We followed the folks to a basement and waited for the all-clear signal. "Welcome to Wisconsin," the hotel lady smiled.

Diep found a public phone and gave her parents a full report, including the thick maroon carpet on the walls of the hotel room and the tornado warnings, of course. *What could I say?* I yanked her from the beautiful weather of the San Francisco Bay Area and brought her to the Midwest to begin my career. *Could this be the worst decision I have made in my entire life?*

Professionally, it was a great start. Indeed, the FPL was a world-renowned research institution and a crown jewel of the Forest Service: every scientist and engineer in the field of wood science and technology vied to be there. Everything one needs to know about wood chemistry, physics, anatomy, identification, engineering properties, pulp, and paper, you name it, comes from there. I was to work with the engineers on the conservation of wood use in housing constructions, including wood mechanics, lumber grading, structural designs, and fire safety.

It was in Wisconsin that I made up for all the years of not fishing in California. With a steady income and no schoolwork, I had time to kill. Once a week, my friend and coworker Vito and I went fishing. We fished the five lakes around Madison; we fished little creeks that zig-zagged through farmers' fields loaded with cow pies, but mostly we fished the Wisconsin River. We caught catfish, white bass, black bass, walleye pikes, and bluegills, sometimes all on the same day. As usual, we stopped by the bait shop in Sauk City on the way for a dozen minnows and a foam cup of nightcrawlers. I found that in Wisconsin, a dozen minnows were never twelve fish. The young bait shop guy reached into the holding tank with a net and scooped out at least a hundred live jumping ones. Somehow, everyone still called it a dozen.

Vito always had a lit cigarette hanging out the corner of his mouth without ever touching it with his hand. One day, he rolled down the car window to flick the glowing butt out onto the highway. A crosswind blew it right back in the car and it landed somewhere between my feet. I slammed on the brakes and the bucket of minnows tipped over. A hundred of them jumped around the car floor as we tried to catch them and put them back in the empty pail. I suppose we never accounted for them all because the car continued to smell like anchovies.

I killed and cooked countless fish and ate them all until Diep put her foot down and yelled, "Please, don't bring any more fish home!" I can't blame her. The kitchen sink turned pink with sticky fish blood. Dry fish scales glittered on the curtains when the moonlight hit the kitchen window. The stench of rotten carcasses in the garbage had drawn wildlife to the house, and even the neighbors complained. I turned my wife into a red meat eater after that.

As a university town, Madison was diverse but nothing like Berkeley. There was one Vietnamese restaurant in the whole city. The Lao supermarket catered to Hmong and Chinese residents and had the basic ingredients we needed but it still lacked many others. Every two months, my wife and I drove three hours to the Vietnamese town in Chicago to buy groceries and send a box of supplies to Ma back home. I had a decent income and we lived comfortably for the first time. However, Wisconsin was not for us. Not only did the cold, long winter bother me, but the cultural isolation overwhelmed us. Diep was homesick for her parents. I missed the Vietnamese community. I was still waiting for an opportunity to go back to Vietnam to see Ma. Working for the U.S. Government now, I couldn't endanger my career while Vietnam was still on the list of sanctioned countries.

Often, we were invited to a coworker's home for Thanksgiving dinner, but not every year. With just the two of us, we didn't bother to cook a turkey and all the fixings. So twice, we had Thanksgiving dinners in the University hospital where Diep practiced nursing as a student. The cafeteria served a good turkey dinner for a few bucks, but the company was deplorable. People were strolling around with IV bags dripping from poles. We drove around a few days during Christmas and found nothing to see but white snowy landscape in all directions. It was time to move.

I rose like a brook trout to a midge when the next fly was cast my way. The Forest Service leadership sent me to Washington, DC for a management job. We sold our little house in Madison and moved to the more balanced climate of the mid-Atlantic states and bought a small townhouse near the Metro Station in Vienna, VA. I started my assignment in the Washington Office in 1992, the year President Clinton arrived at the White House. I was so happy he started normalizing relations with Vietnam and that finally, I could return home legally.

Once I had found Ba, Ma, and my brothers again, my mind was at peace. I focused on my own health and enjoyed leisure time for a change. It was also during this period that I transitioned from bait to fly fishing. My wife's childhood friend Thuy grew up in London and migrated to the U.S. to practice medicine. He spoke English with a Cockney accent, and with his black eyes and sharp jawline looked more like a Korean movie star. Somewhere in the UK, he had picked up fly-fishing and a "catch and release" philosophy—another Vietnamese gone astray!

One evening, Thuy grabbed me and said, "Let's go fishing, mate."

"I have no gear, and I don't know how to throw a clothesline."

"No worries, let me show you." He took me to the golf course behind his house and rigged up. In the dark, we walked like two thieves past the *No Fishing* sign toward the pond that was known to hold huge bass. "I have seen them jump clear out of the water after dragonflies or take a duckling in the spring," Thuy said. As soon as he dropped a bass bug on the dark water, WOOOM! A monster exploded from the weed bed below and splattered water all over us. It then did a dance number above the surface and broke off. I thought of my brother Bê and our fishing the koi in the neighbor's pond. Too bad I couldn't fish with him anymore. He had become a law-abiding citizen after Giải Phóng—a few years with the volunteer army in Cambodia gave him a bad case of Malaria and a deep fear of the Government.

Following Thuy's footsteps, I became Izaak Walton's "Compleat Angler." I invested in fly-rods, reels, vests, waders, fly boxes, boots, and everything the Orvis company advertised in their glossy catalog. I learned to cast with a fly rod and loved the Zen-like back and forward motion of the fly line in the air. I like casting so much that I have not gone back to throwing a weighted lure with a spin rod ever since. I amassed a library of fly-fishing literature, every book written about the art and science of the salmonids. I got myself a vise to tie my own flies. My study became a den of obsession, filled with threads and hackles, peacock herl, rabbit fur, deer hair, cul de canard (ass hairs of a duck), bucktail in many dyed colors, and hooks from mosquito size to one-inch long. The dust and feathers bounced every time the pressure in the house changed abruptly when Diep slammed the door on her way out.

I had many fine outings throughout Maryland and Virginia with Thuy, but with a demanding job as an MD and a baby to tend to, he fished less and less. I got a clear message from the way his wife glared at me that he was not available.

Finding a fishing buddy is not easy. It is about as difficult as finding a life partner: someone you can talk to for hours in a car on the way up the mountain, who only swears once in a while and not for the hell of it, who is not malicious or ill-tempered and will forgive you for your bad habits as well. Having a boat and being able to handle a canoe is a bonus.

A Navy submarine veteran and a canoe racer, my colleague Doug had the physique of an athlete even at the age of sixty-something. We worked out a full-year calendar to fish everywhere within a two-hour drive from DC. We cast for brook trout on our bellies around warm limestone creeks of Pennsylvania in the middle of snowy winters. We floated the Shenandoah and Potomac rivers in the morning fog to cast for smallmouth bass when redbuds and dogwoods bloomed along the banks, and gaggles of Canadian geese zoomed in formation overhead. We paddled the Chesapeake Bay to chase bluefish and stripers (striped bass) in the summer whenever the waves were no more than one foot. Two people fishing in a canoe with nine-foot fly rods can be a recipe for disaster. We had a clear understanding: I would watch my back cast, and he wouldn't whack me in the head with his forward. It was best for me to cast sideways from a sitting position—I perfected the art.

Every Friday in April and May, Doug and I took leave and went fishing for shad. Shad are large herrings, between two and five pounds. Airborne the moment they got hooked, their shiny, scaly bodies shimmered in the morning light, and they swam back downstream with all their muscular ocean-going strength. The DC office joked about our absenteeism as "the shad story." In the dark at 5 am, we were the only ones walking the gravel path to the raging river. We rigged up and climbed huge boulders in the dim morning light to cast into the current, letting the flies drift and sink into deep holes where the fish rested between runs. In just about every cast, a fish would take the shiny shad dart and make its acrobatic jump.

Fishing with Doug was the best, but the time came for him to move to the Pacific Northwest and me back to California. We said goodbye to the rivers back East and headed to the other coast. He often sent me pictures of sea-run cutthroats in the Pacific peninsula. In return, I told him about big juicy rainbow trout in the Upper Sacramento River near Mount Shasta.

Over my thirty-year career with the Forest Service, I was fortunate to be sent to every state in the union. On trips to the "field," I often packed a fly rod with me anywhere there was rumor of fish:

large rainbow trout in Idaho during a Mormon cricket hatch, gorgeous brook trout in mountain streams of the Smoky Mountains, hefty brown trout in Lassen National Park, native rainbows in the Upper Sacramento River, and a few secret locations where the fish biologists in the Forest Service took me.

Hard pressed, I could match anyone at the casting pond with tall tales. I often brag about casting for Dolly Varden in Juneau at 3:00 am one May morning when the sun had already risen. People joke: "Are they the fish that have these two huge... fins?" Well, I am told that the fish got its name after a famous woman whose apron has many colorful dots. Also, in Alaska, I cast tiny midges to rising Arctic grayling in the frozen North Slope, where scientists study the effects of climate change on the permafrost. A small stream emerged from the ground heated by geothermal and maintained an ecosystem full of graylings which taste like thyme, according to those scientists. Once you have seen the beauty of this creature, you would think twice about killing and eating it.

Come to think of it, I am one of a few rare Vietnamese who fly fish and practice catch and release. Ông Ngoại may ask "What? You let a fish go?" However, he may forgive his grandson who left the home village and wandered out to the vast world, acquired a new language, ate strange foods, got fat and bald, spent thousands on expensive gear, caught a fish only once in a while, and let it live.

I have no satisfactory answer for my ancestors or my Vietnamese compatriots. I am among the lucky ones living in America, having a well-paying job, and the choice to fish for recreation and not for food. It is not snobbery. I am not above killing a hatchery trout and frying it in butter and dill weed without a trace of guilt. But I prefer not having to mess with the act of cleaning fish after a hard day on the river. Been there, done that. Like many rivers I have fished, my life has gone through riffles and pools, quiet stretches and turbulent drops, and fly-fishing has soothed my mind and brought me peace. I have enjoyed long hikes in the woods, casting a fluid loop toward the ponderosa pines across the river at a rising trout in the twilight, sharing a bottle of Pinot Noir and a ham and cheese sandwich on the river bank after a day of canoeing with a buddy, fish or no fish.

It was April 2001 when Ma died. I was awakened by the dreaded phone call at 3:00 am. I bought a ticket to go home to Vietnam to say a belated good-bye to her, but had to wait two days before I could get on a plane. Two long days! I threw my gear in the car and headed for a Shenandoah Mountain stream where I knew a trout or two might be lurking. It was just me with a watery world on a clear spring day, putting one foot in front of another with mossy rocks beneath my boots and cold water massaging my legs. I braced myself in the middle of the stream below a fishy-looking riffle ready to deliver a Griffith's Gnat tied on a twelve-foot leader tapered to a fine hair tippet. My mind was clear of clutter, and at that moment, it was tuned like a concert instrument, precise and perfect. I heard my mother's voice in my ears. She said I had done all I could for her, and she didn't want me to be sad. I felt the weight of the line rolling out in the air, carrying with it my regrets, guilt, anger, longings, and finally, when I was ready to let go, the line unfurled and unfurled and cast all that away.

Acknowledgments

I belong to a generation of Vietnamese who became emigrants and refugees around the world. I was among the very lucky few to have left the country before the Fall of Saigon in April, 1975 and escaped the harrowing evacuations in the final days of South Vietnam and the aftermath for years after. However, I could not return to see my family and birthplace for another twenty years.

The stories of the Vietnamese refugees are legion. The deaths and losses during and after the war could fill libraries, yet only a few of my contemporaries are writers and storytellers. Tim O'Brien, Ocean Vuong, Andrew Lam, and Nguyen Thanh Viet are my heroes for their award-winning books—their eloquence and command of the language combined with their unique experiences produced great literature. What is missing to me is the experience of my generation: those of us who came of age in Vietnam during the war in their late teens or as adults. We found a new home and struggled to build a future in a new country. Often, it is just too painful for us to look back, let alone write about the past.

Ten years ago, I began the process of creative writing with a summer course at Berkeley City College with Sharon Coleman. The short six weeks opened a tap and primed the pump for words to flow. The subsequent classes I took with Sharon gave me a writing voice and I started writing these stories which became the book.

This book's title, *Skinny Woman in a Straw Hat,* became solidified one evening when I was face-to-face with the late Berkeley poet Julia Vinograd at a Poetry Express, a poetry venue in Berkeley. We talked about Vietnam and she asked me to describe to her what the country looked like. I drew the map in the air with my hand the shape of the conical straw hat for the north, an S-shaped backbone curve for the coastline, and a belly for the Mekong Delta. She said I should write a poem about that and I did, and then this whole book.

Many friends have added value to this book as I developed the stories and storytelling—serving as readers and giving me valuable feedback. Among them are Patricia Kutza, Jim Barnard, and Gary Turchin in my monthly prose group, and Joy Reichart, writer and coach. Their comments helped me achieve the emotional impacts of the stories.

Two years ago, I made the decision that it was time for this book to be published. I turned again to Sharon Coleman for help. She asked me the most incisive questions, suggested additions where there were gaps, and proposed many reductions in redundancy. The result was a dramatic improvement in every story and the whole book in general.

I am indebted to the Nomadic Press for selecting it for the 2023 publication lineup. Many thanks are due to Nina Sacco of Nomadic Press who worked with me to edit and put the finishing touch on the whole book to make it the best it can be. However, I was saddened when Nomadic went out of business before this book was birthed.

I am happy and honored that Nick Walker, Managing Editor of Autonomous Press, believed in my book and gave it a second chance.

I am thankful to my wife Diep; my brothers living in the U.S. and in Vietnam; companions Gordon, Deb, and Harold from the International Crane Foundation; Dr. Ni of Can Tho University; Titus Peachey, who taught me English when I was a boy in Saigon; boyhood friends Binh and Khanh; and countless friends who fished with me on so many rivers.

Finally, this book is dedicated to Ma, who gave me enough love to last a lifetime.

About the Author

Hao C. Tran left Vietnam as a young man to go to college in Australia and later settled in the United States. Shortly after he left Saigon, the war ended and he couldn't return for 20 years. Since 1994, he has gone back to his homeland a dozen times, and many of his short stories are based on these journeys. Hao's stories are from the perspective of a Việt Kiều, a Vietnamese living overseas. He writes about his own experience as an immigrant, his family, the people he encountered in his travels, and the heart-breaking changes in a post-war Vietnam.